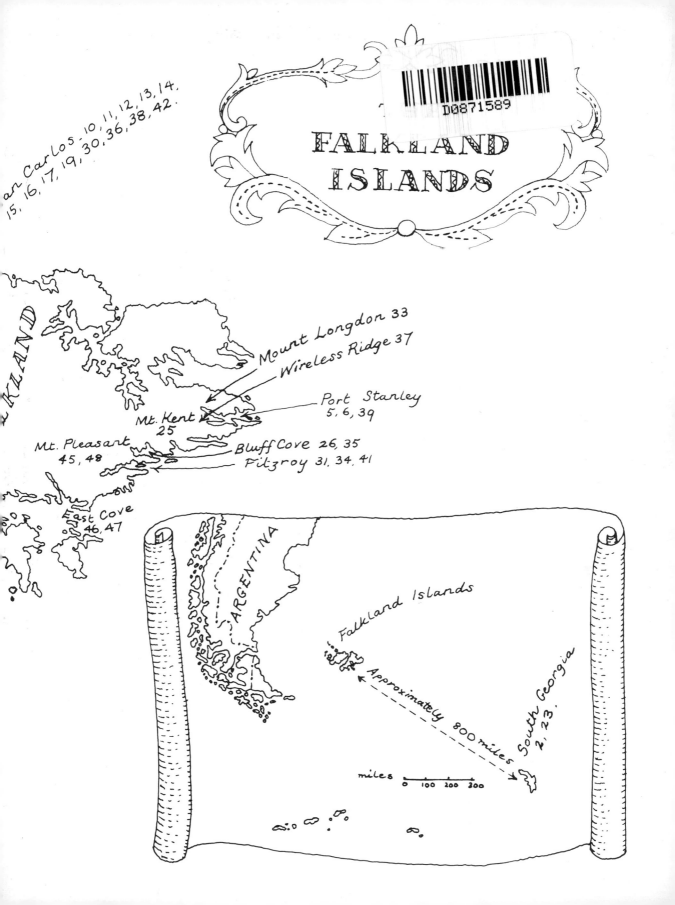

FALKLAND ISLANDS

an Carlos 10, 11, 12, 13, 14, 15, 16, 17, 19, 30, 36, 38, 42.

KLAND

Mount Longdon 33

Wireless Ridge 37

Port Stanley 5, 6, 39

Mt. Kent 25

Mt. Pleasant 45, 48

Bluff Cove 26, 35

Fitzroy 31, 34, 41

East Cove 46, 47

ARGENTINA

Falkland Islands

Approximately 800 miles

South Georgia 2, 23.

miles 0 100 200 300

The Making of a War Artist

San Carlos Water – 24 May 1982
(Oil study 40″ × 26″, purchased by the Royal Naval Museum, Portsmouth)

The Making of
a War Artist

David Cobb:
the Falklands Paintings

Foreword by Admiral of the Fleet Lord Lewin
KG, KCB, MVO, DSC

CONWAY
MARITIME PRESS

For Jean, who had to stay behind

ISBN 0 85177 324 9
First published in Great Britain 1986 by
Conway Maritime Press Ltd,
24 Bride Lane
Fleet Street
London EC4Y 8DR

Typeset by Witwell Ltd, Liverpool
Printed and bound by Butler and Tanner, Frome
Colour section printed by Clark Constable, Edinburgh
Designed by Geoff Hunt

Contents

Foreword

Many of those who have followed the profession of the sea have been tempted to try their hand with paint-brush and pencil. In those days before the camera it was the only way to describe more graphically than the written word the wonders of the newly discovered world or dispositions in battle, while the accurate representation of a coastline and its landmarks was an essential aid to navigators. It became the practice, still followed, to encourage Midshipmen to develop latent talent by requiring them to execute a statutory number of sketches to illustrate their Journals. While inevitably standards of attainment were variable, sailors have always been quick to discern and appreciate the skill of those who can catch the sea in all its moods and truthfully represent ships in all their forms. Small wonder, then, that David Cobb has earned such a high reputation; he epitomises the sailor-artist and his work has long been admired, particularly by those who know and love the sea. He must be uniquely qualified by a combination of artistic achievement, professional understanding and wide experience of war at sea to record for posterity some of the events that occurred during the operations in the South Atlantic.

In time, the historians will allocate that campaign its proper place in our National History and those of us who were involved should not be tempted to rate its importance too highly; but perhaps some personal observations are acceptable. Looking back, once General Galtieri and his Junta had launched their amphibious forces to occupy the Falklands, a military outcome was inevitable. Since neither government could surrender on the vital issue of sovereignty and survive, a negotiated settlement was unachievable. For the British, indeed for the cause of freedom, such aggression – condemned by the United Nations – could not be allowed to go unchallenged.

While Mr Haig shuttled to and fro and the Task Force crawled down the chart of the South Atlantic (or so it seemed to watchers in Whitehall) Argentinian reinforcements poured into the Falklands to multiply the strength of their original garrison by a factor of five or six. Each day brought the Antarctic winter closer. It was not a time for faint hearts. In the event, thanks to a near miracle of logistic improvisation and fighting that was a triumph of training and leadership, the operation achieved all its objectives. Sadly, a thousand men of both nations lost their lives, such is the tragic price of freedom. Many thousands more Argentinians had already died at home for their opposition to the military rule of General Galtieri and his predecessors. The Falkland Islanders now live liberated from the grip of this oppressive regime, and because of defeat, Galtieri has since been ousted and democratic government restored to the Argentinian people. Some of the former leaders now stand trial for crimes against their own countrymen.

Looking further back to similar episodes in our past history – and there are many – I venture to forecast that whatever importance historians may allocate to the operation they are likely to rate both its execution and its consequences highly. As operations go, it was quick, efficient and successful. I find it sad that this clear-cut victory for which our country has every reason to be both proud

7

and grateful should later be blurred by a welter of political point-scoring. More than two hundred years ago General Wolfe, that great practitioner of amphibious operations asked the question that must be in many minds: 'But why this censure when the affair is so happily decided? To exercise one's ill nature?'

There have been many books about the Falklands Campaign, some good, others best left unopened. But this book is entirely different and will be treasured by those lucky enough to own it, to be brought out and browsed over long after all the others are forgotten. With meticulous research, drawing on his feel for the sea, experience of battle and the Falklands terrain and using his considerable artistic skill, David Cobb has depicted and described great events in such a way that those who were there will say 'That is exactly how it was.' All aspects are covered, sea, land and air, from hopeful departure for the unknown through hard-fought action and vital support to triumphal homecoming. Throughout is the constant reminder of all important, all pervading weather factor. Those of use who were left 'abed in England' can be assured; this is how it must have been.

Admiral of the Fleet Lord Lewin KG, KCB, MVO, DSC

Engraved on the plinth of the New Stanley War Memorial

"IN MEMORY OF THOSE WHO LIBERATED US.
14 JUNE, 1982"

ACTIVE	ALACRITY	AMBUSCADE		825 NAVAL AIR SQUADRON
ANDROMEDA	ANTELOPE	ANTRIM	INVINCIBLE	
ARDENT	ARGONAUT	ARROW		801 NAVAL AIR SQUADRON
AVENGER	BRILLIANT	BRISTOL		820 NAVAL AIR SQUADRON
BROADSWORD	CARDIFF	COVENTRY	LEEDS CASTLE	MINERVA	PENELOPE
DUMBARTON CASTLE		ENDURANCE	PLYMOUTH	SHEFFIELD	YARMOUTH
EXETER	FEARLESS	GLAMORGAN	CONQUEROR	COURAGEOUS	ONYX
GLASGOW	HECLA	HERALD	SPARTAN	SPLENDID	VALIANT
HYDRA		INTREPID	GOOSANDER		TYPHOON
HERMES			CORDELLA	FARNELLA	JUNELLA
	800 NAVAL AIR SQUADRON		NORTHELLA	PICT	APPLELEAF

BAYLEAF	ENGADINE	OLMEDA
BLUE ROVER		BRAMBLELEAF
FORT AUSTIN		FORT GRANGE
OLNA	PEARLEAF	PLUMLEAF
REGENT	RESOURCE	STROMNESS
TIDEPOOL		TIDE SPRING
SIR BEDIVERE		SIR GALAHAD
SIR GERAINT		SIR LANCELOT
SIR PERCIVALE		SIR TRISTRAM
ALVEGA		BRITISH ENTERPRIZE III
ASTRONOMER		ATLANTIC CONVEYOR
ATLANTIC CAUSEWAY		ANCO CHARGER
AVELONA STAR		BALDER LONDON
BALTIC FERRY		BRITISH AVON
BRITISH DART		BRITISH ESK
BRITISH TAMAR		BRITISH TAY
BRITISH TEST		BRITISH TRENT
BRITISH WYE	CANBERRA	ELK
CEDAR BANK		CONTENDER BEZANT
EUROPIC FERRY		FORT TORONTO
G A WALKER	IRIS	GEESTPORT
IRISHMAN	LAERTES	LYCAON
QUEEN ELIZABETH 2		NORLAND
RANGATIRA		St BRANDAN
St HELENA	SAXONIA	MYRMIDON
SALVAGEMAN	SAPELE	SANDSHORE
NORDIC FERRY		SCOTTISH EAGLE
SHELL EBURNA		STENA INSPECTOR
St EDMUND	UGANDA	STRATHEWE
TOR CALEDONIA		STENA SEASPREAD
WIMPEY SEAHORSE		YORKSHIREMAN
737 NAVAL AIR SQN		809 NAVAL AIR SQN
815 NAVAL AIR SQN		824 NAVAL AIR SQN
825 NAVAL AIR SQN		829 NAVAL AIR SQN
845 NAVAL AIR SQN		846 NAVAL AIR SQN
847 NAVAL AIR SQN		848 NAVAL AIR SQN
899 NAVAL AIR SQN		

ROYAL MARINES

40 COMMANDO
42 COMMANDO
45 COMMANDO
COMMANDO LOGISTIC REGIMENT
3 COMMANDO BRIGADE
3 COMMANDO BRIGADE AIR SQN
AIR DEFENCE TROOP
1st RAIDING SQUADRON
SPECIAL BOAT SQUADRON
BAND OF HMRM CDO FORCES
Y TROOP
HQ COMMANDO FORCES
MOUNTAIN & ARCTIC WARFARE CADRE

ARMY

THE BLUES AND ROYALS
4th FIELD REGIMENT RA
12th AIR DEFENCE REGIMENT RA
29th COMMANDO REGIMENT RA
43rd AIR DEFENCE BATTERY RA
148 COMMANDO FO BATTERY RA
11 FIELD SQN 38 ENGR REGT
36 ENGINEER REGIMENT
59 IND COMMANDO SQN RE
5th INF BDE HQ & SIGNALS SQN

30th SIGNAL REGIMENT
2nd BN SCOTS GUARDS
1st BN WELSH GUARDS
1st BN 7 DEO. GURKHA RIFLES
2nd BN THE PARACHUTE REGT
3rd BN THE PARACHUTE REGT
22 SAS REGIMENT
656 SQN ARMY AIR CORPS
17 PORT REGIMENT RCT
47 AIR DESPATCH SQN RCT
407 TROOP RCT
16 FIELD AMBULANCE RAMC
9 ORDNANCE BN RAOC
81 ORDNANCE COY RAOC
10 FIELD WORKSHOPS REME
160 PROVOST COMPANY RMP
2 POSTAL AND COURIER REGT RE
6 FIELD CASH OFFICE RAPC
ROYAL SCHOOL OF ARTILLERY SUPPORT REGT
601 TAC PARTY (FORWARD AIR CONTROLLER)
602 TAC PARTY (FORWARD AIR CONTROLLER)
603 TAC PARTY (FORWARD AIR CONTROLLER)

ROYAL AIR FORCE

1(F)	SQUADRON	HARRIER
10	SQUADRON	VC10
18	SQUADRON	CHINOOK
24	SQUADRON	HERCULES
30	SQUADRON	HERCULES
47	SQUADRON	HERCULES
70	SQUADRON	HERCULES
29	SQUADRON	PHANTOM
42	SQUADRON	NIMROD MK1
44	SQUADRON	VULCAN
50	SQUADRON	VULCAN
101	SQUADRON	VULCAN
55	SQUADRON	VICTOR
57	SQUADRON	VICTOR
120	SQUADRON	NIMROD MK2
201	SQUADRON	NIMROD MK2
206	SQUADRON	NIMROD MK2
202	SQUADRON	SEA KING

3 WING HQ UNIT RAF REGT
15 FIELD SQUADRON RAF REGT
63 SQUADRON RAF REGT
1 ACC RADAR
TACTICAL COMS WING
TACTICAL SUPPLY WING
MOBILE AIR MOV SQUADRON
ORDNANCE DEMOLITION UNIT
MOBILE METEOROLOGICAL UNIT
MOBILE CATERING SUP UNIT

ARMY

49 FIELD REGIMENT RA
33 ENGINEER REGIMENT
MILITARY WORKS FORCE RE
14th SIGNAL REGIMENT
602 SIGNAL TROOP
19 FIELD AMBULANCE RAMC
2 FIELD HOSPITAL RAMC
JOINT HELICOPTER SUPPORT UNIT
29 TRANSPORT & MOVEMENT REGT RCT

Acknowledgements

In the tense run-up to the Falkland landings I had only two certainties. I knew from personal experience of small-scale, sea-borne, Commando-type raids in World War II, and from reading history, how prone to disaster are all combined operations involving two or more Services. I knew also to my regret that the web-footed artist, part-seagoer, part-illustrator, (once so common and of which I was just one of many) had virtually disappeared; but if war broke out, I felt sure my sort of work would have a use once more provided I saw the battlefield. I did see it because the Navy arranged with the RAF to fly me out when the Army took me over; but I had no prior contract or commissions as the modern Navy does not commission painters. Certainly I never foresaw this book, its strange format and random assembly so like the Falkland Campaign itself which, if any other nation in the world had tried to plan it in detail, would never have been mounted at all.

The Introduction does what it says; and my Falkland Diary which comes later appears almost verbatim. I wrote it solely for my wife with no idea of publication. I wanted to share with her a vivid experience which unavoidably she missed. As an artist, botanist and war-time Naval cartographer involved in Combined Ops, she would have understood so much.

Nearly every drawing and painting in the book began as a hasty shorthand note for my own use, and the battered state of many is a reminder of the urgent days in the summer and autumn of 1982 when they were done. Because I never foresaw their appearance here, I have not tidied or altered them for publication. This would destroy their integrity. Working drawings and colour ideas they were and must remain, warts and all. Even their reproduction in this book has been by extempore means. Further, many of the paintings, large and small, have been photographed without any of the customary studio facilities, as and when they could be reached. Some, indeed, have had to be printed from my own file of amateur snapshots, with no chance of 'colour-balancing' because the actual painting was 8000 miles away on the bulkhead of a ship off the Falklands, on the wall of an Army Mess in Germany, or locked up for six months to await the return of its owner from Belize. This may upset today's sophisticated readership, accustomed only to the finest reproductions, but at least for anyone interested, this is a record of their existence and ownership.

At the forefront of my mind was a wish to pay tribute to all who worked everywhere to achieve our victory. In a dark world their energy, resource, determination, discipline and bravery shone out like a beacon. In theory their task was impossible, yet they fulfilled it with speed, economy and, in the end, lest it be overlooked, humanity.

Very many people with special knowledge or responsibilities, or both, helped me towards these drawings and paintings. Once again I thank every one of them most warmly. There are a number of others to whom I owe thanks no less sincere. All have tried with varying success to shield me from my grosser follies and generally helped to launch the boat if not actually to man its oars. Some have since retired; others have been decorated, honoured and promoted. For simplicity I refer to most in the rank and style they held in 1982 before the Falklands Campaign. Those whose names have escaped inclusion will, I hope, bear with me now as kindly as when we met.

For over 30 years kind Service friends have kept me in touch with their different professions ashore, and have taken me to sea in their various ships. This ever-generous encouragement has played a much larger part in my life and in the creation of this book than any of them can possibly realise. Admiral of the Fleet Lord Lewin KG, KCB, MVO, DSC, who was Chief of the Defence Staff in 1982 has very kindly contributed a Foreword.

Two other people, also relative strangers, were good enough to read and pass comment on the Introduction. Admiral Sir Henry Leach, GCB, ADC who was First Sea Lord during the campaign, made some invaluable suggestions. Professionally very different was the background of Lieutenant Alistair Bruce of Crionaigh late of the Scots Guards and Tumbledown Mountain, East Falkland. His was the experience and outlook of a new generation of soldiers reported with care and clear perception. I am much in debt to all of them.

In a host of different ways, for so much of it is their story, not mine, I acknowledge the help given to me by the following:

The Countess Mountbatten of Burma, PC, CD, JP,   DL
The Rt Honourable the Earl of Inchape
The Rt Honourable the Lord Shackleton, KG.,   PC., OBE.
Vice-Admiral Sir David Brown KCB.
Vice-Admiral JM Webster
Vice-Admiral Sir Simon Cassels, KCB, CBE
Vice-Admiral Sir Desmond Cassidi, KCB
Rear-Admiral Sir John Woodward, KCB
Rear-Admiral WJ Graham

Commander CRT Craig, RN
Lt Commander CT de Mowbray, RN
FCPO Pughe, RN
Captain R Parsons, MA, RN (retd)
Commander D White, OBE, RN (retd)
Lt Commander N McMillan, RN
Lt Commander N Maddox, RN
Captain R McQueen, RN
Lt T MacMahon, RN
Lt Commander D Mowlam, RN
Commander D Joel, RN
Captain CPO Burne, RN
Commander NJ Tobin, RN
Commander D Hart Dyke, MVO, RN
Lt Commander R Warden, RN
Commander J Castle, RN
Ltd Commander S Thornewill, RN
Captain ESJ Larkin, RN
Major E Southby-Tailyour, RM
Lt Commander M Blissett, RN
Lt Commander N Thomas, RN
CPO MJ Tupper, RN
PO ABT Ashdowne, RN
Captain P Williams, OBE, RN
Captain R Villar, DSC, RN (retd)
Commander GA Smith, RN
Lt Commander M Callaghan, RN
Captain WR Canning, RN
Captain F Grenier, RN
Captain DS Dobson, RN
Commander R Compton-Hall, MBE, RN (retd)

Major-General DC Thorne, CBE
Lt Colonel M Holroyd-Smith, RA
Brigadier JHA Thompson, CB, OBE, RM
Lt Colonel J Smith Bingham, Blues & Royals
Major G Birdwood, Blues & Royals
Captain R Field, Blues & Royals
Lt M Coreth, Blues & Royals
Lt Col D Chaundler, 2 Para
Major C Keeble, 2 Para
Captain J Holborn, 2 Para
Colonel DRP Lewis, Welsh Guards
Lt Colonel J Rickett, Welsh Guards
Captain M Johnson, RA
Major RB Edwards, RA
Lt Colonel KRG Eve, RA
Lt Colonel HWR Pike, MBE, 3 Para
Major RHB Barton, MBE, 3 Para
Major J Tulloch, RA
Major P Shahinian, RA
Major C Gilmour, QOH
Captain D Maitland-Makgill-Crichton, QOH
Lt A Mills, 3 Para

Lt S Whitaker, RA

Charles Tidbury, Esq
John Smith, Esq
Mr & Mrs Richard Cockwell
Colin White, Esq, MA
K Hall, Esq
R Bunning, Esq
Miss Nina Field
Michael Kenny, Esq
Captain DA Ellerby
Captain DJ Scott Masson
Captain JP Morton
Captain JG Clark
Captain HR Lawton
Captain P Johnson
Major General PE de la C de la Billiere, CBE, DSO, MC
Captain C Laurance, RN
Captain J Ferrie, RN
Captain DA Reynolds, RFA
Commander T Millett, RN
Lt Commander C Watkins, RN
Lt S Wilson, RN

Wing Commander B Nicolle, RAF
Flight Lieutenant T Pembrey, RAF
Corporal Love, RAF
WO2 KD Willingale, AAC
Alan Dickson, Esq
P Beck, Esq
D Poppy, Esq
R Vincent, Esq
P Mead, Esq
E Sant, Esq
Oliver Whitehead, Esq
W Bloomfield, Esq
J Stokes, Esq
F Kennedy, Esq
Lt Colonel P Lutter RAMC
W/O M Sterba, RAMC
Gerald Dixon, Esq, Dip ARCH, RIBA, Dip TP
James Hamilton, Esq
Alistair Maclean, Esq

Introduction

In my short life I have never ceased to try to get myself afloat under oars, sail, motor or steam because, it turned out, the sea and ships meant far more to me than anything ashore. When I could not get afloat or in sight of salt water I would try to draw what I had seen as a substitute for the real thing.

This seemed natural to me because in those days, many years before TV, video or even colour photography, the work of British marine artists was much more significant, widespread and better understod than it is today; so too was that of all other creators stirred by the sea, whether they wrote music, prose, history, plays or poetry. All were performing at the very centre of Britain's stage.

To explain my special interest in the Falklands I must go back to before World War II. In 1935 I was a newly-joined Naval Cadet. I knew little about British sea-power, but indisputably I was now part of it.

Inefficient as the Royal Navy warships may have been for land conquest, they were admirably adapted (as Drake had taught and Napoleon and the Kaiser had discovered) for discouraging that ambition in others; or for alleviating its worst accompaniments. As well as being an efficient means of blockade in war, in peace the Navy transposed itself very effectively into a floating embassy, a police force or a philanthropic agency. When tragedy struck, as in the Smyrna massacres, or during the Spanish Civil War of 1936/7, the Navy moved in its nearest ships to succour the hapless refugees. In addition to the Atlantic, Mediterranean and China Fleets, there was a continual round of Naval calls being made upon every country that could be reached by sea. This was called 'showing the Flag' and added to the trade of our huge merchant fleet (we owned half and had built two-thirds of all the world's tonnage) it created a global influence now hard to imagine.

In those days around the seaways of Spithead and the Solent, in the Channel and the Thames, the evidence of British Sea Power was still unavoidably obvious and, whatever its visual effect upon others, in my case the pages at the back of my school exercise books soon began to matter to me far more than those at the front. On these I drew happily and illicitly all the rich variety of ships and craft I had seen. My family's small yachts and others; tramps, cargo ships; multi-funnelled translantic liners, the King's fine old cutter *Brittania* racing against the big class, impressive Royal Navy warships, tugs, sailing barges and fishing trawlers. Not just as profiles, but under way at sea, heeling with sails full of wind or smoke curling down over a yeasty wake astern.

Every maritime civilisation seems to have thrown up people like myself; I am just another in the long line of varied seagoers descended from those prehistoric marine artists, who drew their love for ships and wonder at the sea on the rocks of Scandinavia in the Bronze Age, on painted ceramics of th ancient Mediterranean world on the seaport seals of the mediaeval Channel ports and in many subsequent ways.

Looking back, I was wonderfully lucky to have seen and experienced something of sea affairs when, for a few short years, traces of the old order, shaped by many centuries of ultra-slow development of natural materials, still overlapped momentarily with the new and artificial.

Between the Wars I saw Irish curraghs (essentially skin-boats) in Donegal, Dutch botters of mediaeval shape fishing under sail in the now-vanished Zuyder Zee, and fast, graceful, cross-channel steam-packets which looked like miniature transatlantic liners were visible from the school playing fields. I spent time aboard the coasting schooner *Elizabeth Drew* (once a Western Ocean craft built at Padstow in 1871 in which Cook could have sailed) and wheedled my way onto the steam tugs which worked out of Newhaven. I cruised and latterly raced offshore, under varied sail and power, across to Belgium and Holland, and once I went up the thriving, busy Thames to Battersea aboard a 'flat-iron' collier, helping to lower the funnel under the bridges. Slowly I began to absorb the history of all these vessels and to make models of some of them; while for nine months of the year Pangbourne trained me for a Naval career – a plan which was ended abruptly by a splintering crash when playing rugger.

At midnight on 11 August 1939 when our little family cutter, bound for Cornwall, was nearing the Eddystone, my brother and I watched, absorbed, as there swished close past us a tall rectangular shape. She was to prove to be the Clyde-built, four-masted barque *Archibald Russell* loaded with grain from Australia, bound from Falmouth for Hull to discharge what was to be her very last cargo, and signalling the end of four centuries of world trade in deep-water square-riggers. It proved an apocalyptic experience, like having seen the damned 'Flying Dutchman,' that sure precursor of disaster foretelling what, a month later, everyone had sworn could and should never happen; but it did. Within only a generation, much of the world embarked on a second and even bloodier war from which its recovery still hangs in the balance. The first was caused by German militarism; and the second was largely contributed to by British pacificism. It was as if mankind himself remained accursed by endless headwinds. Unable ever to gain the peace of port, he is condemned to roam the seas of his existence.

'...Dutch botters of medieval shape...'

'...four masted barque *Archibald Russell* loaded with grain from Australia...'

1 War and Peace

When the Second World War broke out, at first nothing would persuade the Admiralty to accept a salt-stained zealot once more in full health and already attuned to Naval discipline. I was too young, they said. I would be notified, they said. Nothing at all happened. Young and impulsive as I was, for one of my background and consuming interests, this was hard to bear.

Almost overnight came Dunkirk, and my Brighton beach-boat friends were ordered to sail for the beaches and a harbour which I knew (and they didn't) just half an hour before the time they had told me to join them as a spare hand. This was doubly frustrating; but it was soon followed by the national call for volunteers upon all who had experience of small craft. Within an hour I had banished my Cambridge BSc (for ever as it turned out) and was into a train for Chichester. On the familiar Hard at Itchenor I found two RNVR Officers standing on the jetty commandeering motor-yachts for service, staring perplexedly at the few which had been fitted out.

'Do you know any of these boats?' asked the taller of the two. 'Yes' I said unhesitatingly. 'All of them. Every single one.' It was true. For years I'd known and loved their wide variety. 'Are any ready for sea?'. '*Iere*' I said, and pointed her out, moored just above the Sailing Club. (I knew I was safe on that score).

'Could you ferry her round to Hamble?' Certainly I could. I relished handling craft, but it was a dizzy prospect. The immaculate, best-built and -engined yacht of her size in Chichester Harbour, delivered within seconds into the care of David Cobb. I was skipper, mate and engineer. George Noyce ran over the powerful, smooth sleeve-valve Kelvins with me, then returned ashore. Nobby Clark, on the foredeck (later to return to Itchenor to resume his employment) dropped the mooring buoy, and we were swiftly away.

The Royal Naval Patrol Service Depot at Hamble, working to all hours aboard the old steam-yacht *Melisande* needed everyone they could get. They lost no time in taking over this excellent motor-yacht and enlisting its jubilant young skipper.

From early June 1940, with increasing hordes of Luftwaffe opposed by the valiant 'Few' overhead and soon with Dover under shell-fire, until the German plan to land on the Kent coast faded with the approach of winter, I had charge of this 45-foot craft. Eric, Arthur and I (men dressed as seamen) soon painted her Naval grey all over, with the number '16' in white on her bow. At her stern she proudly flew the White Ensign. Based first at Dover, and then at Ramsgate, she was one of a small group of Dunkirk-type 'Little Ships' which formed a chain of primitive Royal Naval auxiliary patrols crewed by fishermen, pilot-boat hands and the like.

Nightly they took up station offshore at fixed points between Reculvers and Dungeness, armed for total war with a .300 Ross rifle, a Hotchkiss machine-gun (both of World War I), a shaded signal torch and six outsize rockets. Until we sighted the enemy and fired our rockets we were forbidden to slip our anchor to get under way. Our prime duty was to signal the approaching of the invasion flotillas; only then to do what damage we might to the enemy. Our ancestors such as the 'sea-fencibles', equally ill-prepared and expendable I dare say, at intervals throughout our island history have kept similar watch; and 1940 ashore or afloat, was no moment to lie abed in England.

When the patrols were withdrawn I was commissioned and sent to serve in convoy escorts in the Atlantic. There I saw illustrated yet again the lesson that Britain never seems to learn; namely, that she is an island power which can survive only as long as others are afraid to attack her or her interests. A fact which is true today as it ever has been, or ever will be.

My introduction was via the famous working-up base at Tobermory, HMS *Western Isles* which became perhaps the most potent Naval factor in the Battle of the Atlantic. There all newly-commissioned Naval escort-ships in the years to come spent a tense fortnight being drilled relentlessly in the rudiments of their job by one of the best-known Naval Officers of World War II. Commodore Stephenson (a retired Vice-Admiral known as 'Monkey Brand') was famously formidable and I was one of his first Midshipmen RNVR, but despite some of the astonishing decisions I took, he gave me every encouragement. Soon I had charge of the 115-ton diesel yacht *Martinetta* which the training programme kept hard at work off Ardnamurchan and in the Minches until, three months later, I was 20 and became a Sub-Lieutenant before being appointed with breath-taking speed as First Lieutenant of HMS *Canna*, a new A/S M/S Atlantic escort trawler.

During the hundreds of ensuing hours of anxious watch-keeping and occasional alarms, I saw ships in convoy of many sorts and nations on every bearing at every range, in every type of climate, and weather, at every hour of day and night. Slow convoys had the compensation that they gave one plenty of time to observe, but strong weather could scatter the low-powered ships far and wide, making them difficult to shove into bed once they had fallen out. Over the ship's broadcast system the distant chimes of Big Ben warbled and crackled from a battered London that in the night in mid-Atlantic seemed infinitely remote.

'...appointed with breath-taking speed as First Lieutenant of HMS *Canna*...'

Memorably picturesque and impressive as Atlantic convoy work proved to be, I shall never forget my first sight and the scent, after a blacked-out, beleaguered England, of Gibraltar aglow with lights on a warm Levanter evening with the famous warships of Force 'H' alongside.

Eighteen months after HMS *Canna* and various vicissitudes, a comprehending cherubim on the wing one day in the offices of the Second Sea Lord's department in Queen Anne's Mansions hovered, momentarily, over a file of Officers' Re-appointments on somebody's empty desk. (Actually his name was Lt George Hemming RNVR, of blessed memory, with whom I had served at Ramsgate) and it led me first to the command of three varieties of short MTBS (as Motor Torpedo Boats were then called). Finally from the autumn of 1944, as one of half a dozen MTB Control Officers embarked aboard the 'trout-line' of frigates in the Southern North Sea, I guided the fortunes and battles of dozens of others in the closing stages of the war in Europe.

These small warships were very exacting. Only some 70 feet long, very fast and highly stressed, they asked much of their crews.

Without proper pre-war development or training, once France had fallen, these few, nascent, nocturnal MTBs and MGBs were the only wholly-offensive blockading surface units which the Navy could deploy against the coast of Europe. Their role recalled the 'cutting-out' sorties of Nelson's day. In time their numbers and size increased and, like the bulk of the wartime Navy, they were manned and commanded by volunteers and reservists who, very early on, merged imperceptibly with regular serving personnel. My first MTB appointment was not until late 1942, so I was a late initiate into this special club, but as an essentially small boat man, I felt immediately at home.

'...very fast and highly stressed, they asked much of their crews...'

Winter in the 'short boats' (which privately held themselves to be the only true believers and at times certainly suffered for their faith) could be harsh indeed. Through deepening dusk, long, weary, often-fruitless nights of mist, moon, starlight, frost, rain, wind and spray, through to dawn, a Commanding Officer and his Coxswain stood side by side; often they were soaking wet and cold in the tiny open bridge. The crew of 10–13 men, whether similarly exposed to the elements on deck, or shut down below nursing delicate, noisy machinery, were at Action Stations and warily alert. Everyone depended on everyone else. Each of us strained to be the first to see or hear, and to act. Close by we could see the loom of Peter's boat, or Mark's, or Mac's, just visible against the night sky.

Wherever it occurred, on the high seas, in the Channel or the North Sea, engaging the enemy was hardly the moment for aesthetics; but at night especially the vivid scenes and colours which were the usual result were imprinted on my mind, though I had no skill or time to paint them. When it all ended I was not quite 24. A year later I had collected my war gratuity. My back wound seemed mended (it wasn't really); now to catch up on life.

By this time I was suffering from acute visual indigestion; and since I foresaw no career in this type of craft in a peace-time Royal Navy, instead I would try to draw and paint what I had learned and seen, and what I hoped to see afloat. I had no cushion of private means, no training, nor any grasp of how to sell work to earn me a living (that is the difficult part of being an artist); but as I was no longer responsible for a lot of lives and ships in action, my own

MTBs on passage.

survival was no worry. Despite this relaxed approach to the matter I had few illusions about our chaotic world, fleeting fame or acquiring a fortune, so perhaps my feet still were fairly near the ground. I numbered one or two very worthwhile Naval and Merchant seamen among my distant forebears; so I would try to reflect their contribution by becoming a painter of our sea affairs.

Our nation had built itself upon its sea-power and a (not ignoble) policy of freedom for all to trade across the seas. It needed no genius to see that even with the recent whole-hearted support of our cousins overseas, our allies in Europe and finally that of the USA this freedom and every other (whose cause Britain had for long months championed single-handed) had only narrowly survived its most brutal threat in world history. Now that an uneasy peace was restored, and because I sensed that England, for all its faults, had fostered and still guarded something that I felt the world could not afford to lose, I would try to illustrate that theme. It seemed a modest but worthwhile aim.

Naive and pretentious as all this may appear, it made sense to me then. In many ways it does still; after all, it was what one had been fighting for. Anyway I knew what I felt even if, like faith, it was difficult to analyse and impossible to explain.

At the outset my work was, naturally, all to do with the sea. Indeed, I knew little about anything else. In time hard-won drawing and painting commissions took me round the main British ports, to the Mediterranean, Germany and Spain, and as I slowly gained experience, the marine aspect had others added to it. Once I painted for Whitbreads a series of pictures illustrating weather-patterns as indicated by clouds, one scene of which took me back into mid-Atlantic aboard a Hastings of the RAF; a wholly fascinating, eight-hour, meteorological and Naval pilgrimage. Later, both the Royal Engineers and the RASC (now the Royal Corps of Transport) asked me to paint scenes abroad connected with their World War II service, and these I found extremely interesting, especially the unique, spearhead role of the Assault Sappers in 1944 in the Normandy landings. Each painting involved learning a wholly new technical subject. In the 1970s I did a series of major paintings to show the revolutionary new methods of container-cargo-handling for the Port of London Authority. From the outset I found my sea knowledge and line-drawing technique of the greatest help in maintaining a flow of work by which to live. For example, in the early 1950s the *Radio Times* had begun to telephone me late on a Friday afternoon, blandly asking if I was working that weekend. Naturally, I was. Did I know this particular ship, or that episode of sea history? Well, as it happened, yes, I did. Could I do a drawing to reach them by Monday morning's first post? Yes, indeed I could!

'One of our Submarines' (*Radio Times* 1955).

Regularly for over 25 years I drew and wrote freelance for the sailing Press and other periodicals at home and abroad on a wide variety of past and present sea affairs. Various editors gave me a very free hand, and great fun it was. With so much to learn and to draw I never contemplated teaching just to earn; nor would I paint pot-boilers, however rewarding they were to the stereotyped demands of a single dealer or printer. Independence or freedom, call it what you will, (some might say obstinacy) meant everything.

All my clients at home and from overseas shared one characteristic which I think I took for granted at the time when they first commissioned me. Without exception these hundreds of different people of every sort for whom I have had the pleasure of working have been absolutely charming; so it disturbs me that I cannot possibly keep in touch with them all.

I drew and painted for individuals; for shipping companies, government organisations and firms of all kinds, publishers, advertising agents, the Armed Services and their museums. For Vospers in the 50s and 60s I used my experience of their war-time short MTB to interpret from blueprints how Peter du Cane's brilliant new high-speed designs would look when built and under way. That was a particularly warm and enjoyable association. It lasted actively for nearly twenty years and continued in friendship. Meanwhile the sea-fever which started it all grew no less. In fact it had become even worse. For the last six years of war I had had to obey orders – as soon as they were over I could issue my own.

Proposed Vosper FPB.

Being stirred by the sea and ships and their history rather than by art (of which I knew little and viewed as a means, not an end) I had long had another urgent post-war aim. To widen my experience I wanted to live afloat, and to cruise single-handed. Accordingly I spent my entire savings on *White Heather*, a shapely, spacious 13-ton gaff-cutter, already well-stricken in years when first she was raced offshore in the 1930s by the Rear-Commodore of the Royal Ocean Racing Club, with his crew of four and a paid hand.

No sooner was I her proud young owner in 1946 than suddenly I found myself possessed also of a highly-desirable and very sporting wife. Her ability as an artist was as large as mine was small. There was only one answer. These two charmers would have to amalgamate; and they did. The three of us migrated to Newlyn in Cornwall, where my wife and I lived and worked most happily for the next seven years before finally moving ashore.

White Heather proved a splendid family home for us and, in due course, our small daughter. Each summer the three of us cruised across to Brittany. This was the peak of enjoyment. For a few blissful weeks, Cinderella-like, outwardly we became rich yachtsmen, and nobody could tell we weren't. That made it even more fun.

Some of *White Heather*'s inventory is worth recalling. It symbolised her ample and diverse character. In her galley we inherited (and still have) a massive willow-pattern meat-dish, adequate for a large turkey; also a pair of handsome plated boot-horns (of military origin, I fancy) and on her cabin coal-stove stood a polished copper kettle. Aloft she carried on an immense mast some 900 feet of sail based on the first Laurent Giles-designed, long-luff gaff-topsail later to be immortalised by the famous *Dyarchy*. Stretched to the end of her 16-foot bowsprit was a huge Yankee jib alleged to have been once the working jib from a 12-metre of the type that races today for the America's Cup. She resembled a small Revenue Cutter, and we loved her most dearly. So did all others (and they were many and famous) who had cruised and raced aboard her.

The next yacht we owned after coming ashore in 1954 was a deliberate contrast; the 1911 Mylne-designed 8-metre *Alpenrose* – a lean, exquisite, 42-foot, classic day-racing yacht of ineffable grace and alarming speed. Darling that she was, she was quite unsuited for the family cruising which we did, had

'...*White Heather*, a shapely, spacious 13-ton gaff cutter...'

'...the 1911 Mylne-designed 8-metre *Alpenrose*...'

no engine and little need of one. To look at, she was a beauty; and to sail her was a privilege. For five exciting seasons we rejoiced in the virtual certainty that whatever sail of our size we sighted ahead on the same course would eventually finish up astern. Her narrow, insecure flush decks, devoid of lifelines, put me in mind of today's sailboards but on a vast scale, to which one hung precariously when changing sail at sea.

Next came the stately 21-ton cutter *Golden Vanity* who with her high bulwarks and fidded topmast, defied every advance in design or rig since 1860 and long before. Like *White Heather* she was a 'gentleman's yacht' and, like so many at the time, of working outline. In her palmiest days she had at one time belonged to the Royal Yacht Squadron when she carried two paid hands in her fo'c'sle. She had been built in 1908 as 'a large singlehander' by the marine artist Arthur Briscoe for himself, his wife and his daughter; so it was satisfying that (once again) after a long absence from the Royal Cruising Club she should be brought back to it by another member, this time also a marine artist, to be crewed by his wife and daughter. Briscoe planned her as a floating studio on the lines of a big Plymouth hooker, with seven feet of headroom, so she was in this respect uniquely suitable for me.

Bought in a spirit of enquiry, a sort of one-man research, the two traditional craft, *White Heather* and *Golden Vanity*, taught me about the seamen and shipwrights of those times when earlier vessels basically like them had worked around much of the globe. The engineless metre-boat *Alpenrose* becalmed in the dark among the rocks and tearing tides of the Brittany coast, was a lively reminder of just how difficult it must have been. By the time we owned them all three were already old pieces of history and, by today's standards, unmanageable; too big, too slow or too fast; and each, at times, was an exciting handful for just two of us; but they were all colossal fun, and on our tight budget we kept them as polished and smart as we possibly could. At the masthead of each in turn I flew appropriately the burgee of the Royal Cruising Club (as both the marine artists Pears and Briscoe had before me) and the coasts we explored in them were then still remote, tranquil and lovely, peopled by fishermen and farmers with seldom another yacht to be seen.

During this time I saw the last of the Breton sailing tunnymen off the Isle de Groix and Concarneau, Greek (or maybe Turkish) caiques in the Aegean, Maltese dshaisas, Scandinavian double-enders off Göteborg and, most exciting of all, in 1977 I made what I believe was a discovery of my own. At least I had read of it nowhere else in learned sea journals.

On the North Spanish coast the local Basque populace, those tough seafarers identified and respected by the Romans, now free at last from Franco's 40-year tyranny, were racing enthusiastically over the Biscay swell in long, open, 14-oared boats each steered by their *padron* with a single oar. Direct descendants they proved to be (and charming ones too) of the mediaeval Basque whalers who had pioneered the whale fishery of all Europe. (The cheering supporters were unbothered by maritime history. They just wanted their crew to win, to collect their substantial bets). My varied sea delights such as these have never ceased. They have ranged from sea-going, and, latterly, flying with the Navy to going up the historic Bosphorus to Istanbul on the bridge of the liner *Nevasa*; and from sea-trials aboard the 50-knot 'Brave' Class Fast Patrol Boats to crewing aboard *Thalatta*, that queen of all the surviving Thames barges. To

'...the stately 21-ton cutter *Golden Vanity*...'

South Stack, Anglesey.

paint such things is the only way I can tell others what I feel about them.

To be sure, mine has been a solitary style of private life, but artists are often like that. Besides, being married to someone of similar disposition we have been very far from lonely. The overriding concerns in each of our lives have been naturally, our current commissions. By these alone we lived. As far as I thought about the matter (for I was never an intellectual) happiness in life seemed to come about through finding out what (legally!) one wanted to do, and then doing it with all one's might. Neither of us have found any difficulty about that. We have both worked like beavers at things that interested us. We still do. We've had a marvellous time.

Between 1950–1975 the pace of change afloat accelerated even more. Almost the whole range of traditional British ships and craft, already much depleted, became fit only for the museum where one or two languish today. Sad silent ghosts they seem to me, devoid of life and warmth (they don't even *smell* right) but the best that we can do. The vast majority which fed us, created our wealth and defended us vanished totally.

'...the pace of change afloat accelerated even more.'

21

2 1977–82

One sunny morning in later May 1944, when I was commanding a hard-working 'short' Motor Torpedo Boat operating in the Channel, I was most unexpectedly given the almost-bizarre responsibility of embarking on the following day the First Sea Lord, Admiral of the Fleet Sir Andrew Cunningham, and Rear Admiral Ramsay, planner of the Normandy invasion. My instructions were to conduct them on a review of the massive D-day fleet of landing ships and others then assembling in the Solent and Spithead.

Thirty years later, in 1971, long after all such Royal Navy MTBs had vanished, I was asked to write a brief history of the Vosper 70ft boat, which brought home to me that this duty could be seen as a unique trust for a young Reservist Commanding Officer, his crew, their ship, but, most of all, for their branch of the Services. I sought to portray that scene with HM MTB *246* wearing the Union Flag, probably the smallest-ever Flagship of an Admiral of the Fleet on the eve of a great sea battle. Some day the subject might interest somebody in the Royal Navy, of which both admirals had been such distinguished servants, and which I admired so greatly.

It so happened some years later that the 'somebody' was Captain J Pack, OBE, at that time Director of the Royal Naval Museum, Portsmouth. He wanted that picture to commemorate a unique event, and I wanted the Museum to have it, so we agreed from the start.

When I showed him my picture it started a discussion which soon began to range happily over the Naval centuries and when at last I came to leave, I felt I had found exactly the right place for it. Out in the stream, beyond the Signal Tower of the Dockyard, lay moored the old Napoleonic frigate *Foudroyant*, the youth training ship of which I had been a Governor for a number of years; close by towered the masts of HMS *Victory*, symbols both of a great sea heritage.

The 1977 Fleet Review.

Meanwhile, in and around Portsmouth and at the Admiralty, the Royal Navy was preparing to stage the following year a scene in Spithead with which they have saluted their Kings and Queens for centuries past.

This was the 1977 Silver Jubilee Fleet Review; and, by the great kindness of Naval friends I was enabled to visit HMS *Cleopatra* and, later, to watch the Review from HMS *Tiger*. This happened just 42 years after King George V's Silver Jubilee Review which I had watched as a 14-year old Cadet aboard the World War I light cruiser HMS *Curacoa* and my feelings had not changed one bit. Meanwhile, invisibly, a major artistic project began to shape itself, and on a scale I would never have imagined.

Following my meeting with Jimmy Pack and in due time (my longest six months ever!) I was commissioned by the Trustees of the Royal Naval Museum to plan and execute a series of paintings, (there were 49 in the end) of the whole course of World War II at Sea, to be hung in the new galleries then planned. Unconsciously, perhaps, my enthusiasm laid this egg: if so, Jimmy's certainly hatched it.

Historically I was doing nothing new. Paintings and sculpture had been used world-wide to record sea affairs of every kind for thousands of years, but the first marine artists to bring ashore on accurate and abundant portrayal had been the Van de Veldes father and son. So able were they and so rich the vein they struck that they remain unsurpassed. How they did it (and, for me, there is still no better way) is well-explained by the Admiralty's directive to Admiral Russel-Shovell dated 18/28 May 1694 to

. . . cause Mr Van de Velde and a servant to be born in victualls on board such ship as he desires . . .

. . . whereas Mr William Van de Velde is appointed by this Board to goe aboard their Mat's Fleet this summer in order to make from time to time draughts and figures or imitations of what shall pass and happen at Sea by battle or fight or the Fleet, you are therefore hereby required and directed to cause him the said William Van de Velde and one servant to be born in victualls only, on Board Such Ship or Ships of ye said fleet as he shall desire to proceed in, and that he be accomodated with such convenience as can be afforded him for ye better performance of this service.*

Despite the revolutionary impact of the nineteenth century camera upon all visual art, the need for graphic artists of all kinds had revived unexpectedly in the middle of the First World War because it was found that newfangled photography made every stretch of tortured Flanders look the same.

At sea it was, and remains, difficult if not impossible to photograph tactical situations successfully, with the ships in the wrong place; the distances too great; and the wide sea much too wide. A camera in close-up is unequalled at counting portholes, or noting mechanical details instantly; but it can distort perspective, shape and proportion. Consequently such subjects have remained the province of the sea-bred sea-painter.

---

*(This quotation was deftly provided by my friend Mark Myers, a skilled seaman and learned marine artist, the moment he heard that I had been commissioned to assemble this book).

The Museum gave me a very free hand over planning the series which covered in stages the main theatres of war, Atlantic, Mediterranean and Pacific. Among the many claims to notice of varied types of ship and service I gave full emphasis to the new and vital role of air-power, and to the part played by Combined Operations, so that all three Services and the Merchant Services were represented.

In early March 1982, this series of paintings was generously given a magnificent unveiling in London by Whitbreads in the foyer of their Porter Tun Room, then housing the huge Overlord Tapestry recording the landings in Normandy. Countess Mountbatten, who has so gallantly assumed the mantle of her famous father, Admiral Lord Louis Mountbatten, launched the exbibition, which was attended by a distinguished and mainly Service audience. Almost immediately after this event the Falklands erupted. The shooting began, the islands were invaded, and many of the guests departed at speed for their posts of duty.

Evacuation of Crete – *Orion* under air attack.

Capture intact of U-boat 570, 27 August 1941.

24

3 The Falklands

Events after the opening of my exhibition in London, began to move with blurry speed, the most public one, the sailing of HMS *Hermes* and HMS *Invincible* from Portsmouth, caught the public imagination and stirred their feelings as only an imminent battle can. Simultaneously there was a huge effort behind the scenes to take up Merchant Ships from trade, to modify, equip, load and despatch the formidable number of vessels needed to support the Assembling Task Force.

Happily we had no bothersome allies to consult; moreover, with the benefit of hindsight, it seemed clear that the Royal Navy, at least, was seeing far ahead, and it was with their timely assembly of this supporting Fleet that by lucky chance I now became involved.

General Haig, the United States Secretary of State, embarked too late upon his diplomatic shuttle. The shooting war which Argentinia had started could not afford to stop. But whatever lay ahead Naval friends were good enough to give me the chance to study the massive preparations needed to repossess the Falklands. In response to reports of shipping movements (which often came to me with only a few hours, or even less, notice) I spent day after day in Southampton and Portsmouth watching and drawing the progress of work. The pace was electrifying; but this type of situation was what I had long tried to prepared myself for.

On one occasion I boarded the Roll-on-Roll-off Ferry, *Tor Caledonia*, at 10.30 in the morning at Southampton, to find her virtually empty and her refuelling modifications far from complete. By 9.00 pm that night she had loaded the long rows of covered anti-aircraft Rapier Fire Units (as I had decided they were) from the quay, plus a mass of other equipment, and had sailed for Ascension Island for onward routeing for the Falklands. She then met a tanker at a rendezvous in the Channel, and steaming close to the other vessel (contrary to all Merchant Service practice and training) successfully tested her fuel replenishment gear.

Tor Caledonia converted.

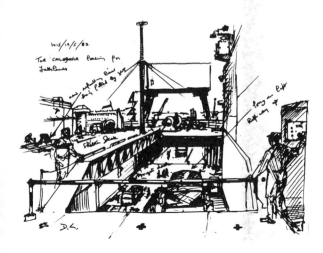

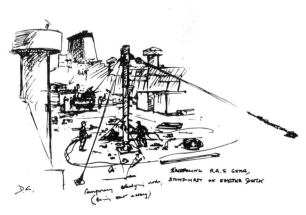

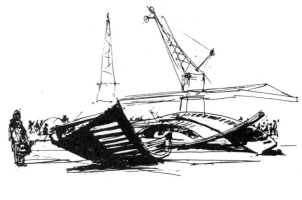

Tor Caledonia, main deck.

'. . .great slices of promenade
shelter-bulwarks. . .'

Though I was carrying out the duty of one, I had no appointment as an
official War Artist (Linda Kitson was to have that honour); indeed, all had
ceased to exist 40 years earlier. The Service people who now helped me did so
unofficially; but their active kindness was very heart-warming. They had
plenty to bother about without me. For my part, I felt I had the unique chance
to say, however humbly, what I felt about them. In truth I was very proud to be
doing something which might, one day, be of historical interest and was
determined not to miss this unique and splended opportunity to serve in the
only way I could. To be sure there was no certainty that the work would ever
be used; indeed, I hoped fervently that it would not. Anyone with or without
experience of war would surely feel the same.

Soon I wanted to make a sketch of *QE II* as she sailed from Southampton on
12 May, and was given a pass to get into the Docks. She was berthed alongside
the old Ocean Terminal, and when I walked through it onto the quayside, I
stared, fascinated, at the great slices of promenade shelter-bulwarks which, in
a matter of hours, the shipwrights from Vosper–Thornycroft had cut off the
ship to clear the way for building the after helicopter-deck. Long, curved,
perforated metal plates with windows along them lay piled at random on the
quayside, like that quizzical form of art which reveals so much more about the
observer and the mad world he has invented for himself than about the artist
who drew it. (Where else could a painter get such ideas? – he's only an
ordinary mortal).

I spent the morning ashore, high up in the Control Tower on the dockhead,
drawing these drastic modifications to the ship. Later I went aboard to be
shown the forest of steel joists which had sprouted overnight beneath this new
landing-deck, to distribute the strain of a big helicopter thumping down onto it
in a South Atlantic gale. From the bridge I drew the new forward helicopter
deck. Meanwhile the alleyways and cabins of the ship were crowded with
Scots and Welsh Guardsmen and Ghurkas who were now embarking from the

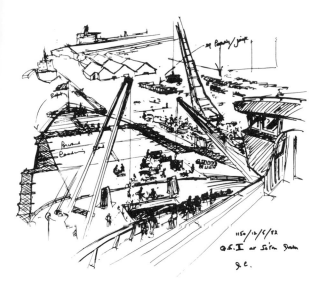

QE 11 at Southampton Docks.

quayside. All were being exhorted to handle their arms with care, to avoid damage to the veneers and furnishings – a strange introduction to war indeed.

The little exploratory oil-sketch that I made ashore from the roof of the Control Tower had a wholly fortuitous result. Very seldom can anyone paint at sea, for obvious reasons, but on this occasion I was on dry land, so, for convenience, I loaded a panel into the lid of my paint-box (it is designed to carry three small panels 12″ × 16″) and went to work. I wanted to catch the mood of the astonishing scene; also, I would have the basis of a larger painting should the need arise. The scope of such a little exploratory oil sketch proved ideal for assembling or re-arranging the many facts I was to be given in the months to come, and to see for myself in the Falklands. Small, handy, easily-altered or happily discarded, such sketches allowed me to develop quickly, sometimes in a few minutes, a variety of different subjects in a small space. So far I have painted some sixty or so, covering the widest possible spectrum of Falkland War subjects. All of them started like reminders sketched on a telephone pad or the back of a menu, so they should not be confused with the much larger commissioned works which only developed later; moreover, their subsequent printing photography has often been handicapped and their surface scarred or imperfect, due to rough handling or other cause.

I reflected as I worked in the ensuing weeks that this war, because of its speed, localised-brevity and small scale created a dramatic standard of its own. Somehow it distressed one's mind even more than total war, when a heavy convoy loss, a town captured or dozens of planes shot down, were all just another day of gain or loss. Perhaps this was caused by one's utter inability to do anything to help.

In the darkness of 21 May, eight days after the *QE II*, sailed from Southampton the initial Landing Force was put ashore in San Carlos Water, East Falkland, by the Navy, Royal Fleet Auxiliaries and Merchant Service.

A mere seven weeks had passed since the islands had been invaded.

4 Getting to the Battlefield

The subsequent recovery of the Falklands was a daring military venture, theoretically impossible and achieved at a remarkably small cost in lives. Struggling to cope with a supply shortage which continually imperilled their whole effort, the outnumbered initial Landing Force faced a problem stark indeed, for the military dictum was that only control of the air and a three-to-one superiority of ground forces might allow of their success in an opposed landing.

Whatever in the country had changed outwardly, it showed the temper of the nation's Armed Forces and Merchant Service to be unaltered. In vision, decisiveness and professionalism it smacked of Wolfe at Quebec or Hawke at Quiberon; and will surely take its place among the country's most noteworthy minor campaigns.

As far as possible ships, including warships in the amphibious operating area of San Carlos Water, the selected landing area, were positioned close to high points of land, close inshore, to minimise the aiming time of attacking aircraft. This shrewd tactic largely paid off, and many of the fuses on the Argentinian bombs had insufficient time in flight to become armed before the moment of impact. Despite day-long attacks, the entire initial Landing Force was put ashore without the loss of a single life; and this Naval triumph was the prelude to a military victory ashore introduced by Goose Green, every bit as accomplished.

Understandably these activities in far distant South Georgia and the Falklands, of which few people knew anything at all, were very difficult for the public to follow. Their hitherto-trusty source of news and pictures, TV was out of action on two counts. Technically transmission was not possible but, anyway, censorship would have stopped it. You do not show your plans to the man who is shooting at you. This conflict of aims must divide any forces that are at war from the media who want to report their progress.

A new generation in Britain who had enjoyed unbroken peace was now to be reminded once more that in war, as in love, to win is all that counts; but as often happens in war the more significant reports which indicated success were less newsworthy than local losses of ships or aircraft. Yet in war all gains cost something, and lives are unavoidably lost.

If any nation should have understood that cost and, however sadly, paid it uncomplainingly, even proudly, it was the democratic British. Their civilised lives derived solely from their forefathers' successful exercise of sea-power, the determination to defend their priceless freedoms, and by sheer luck (not foresight) just enough amphibious specialist force left in 1982 to support their beliefs in the Falklands. (For example our new HMS *Invincible*, one of the two essential Carriers, was all but sold to Australia.) The margins were pitifully narrow: often there were none.

Soon afterwards, the return of the *QE II* on 11 June from South Georgia posed new problems. Having delivered 5 Brigade she was bringing home the survivors and casualties of *Coventry*, *Antelope* and *Ardent*, and I wanted to learn some details. This was a delicate but urgent matter; once they had dispersed on survivors' leave I could hardly disturb them.

It was a perfect summer morning as we approached the great ship off Portland Bill. We were aboard a Royal Navy Wessex carrying press men and photographers despatched to cover the first such personal interviews available to them.

Perhaps the unusual experience unsettled my companions; or perhaps I was over sensitive to the presence on board *QE II* of the survivors and wounded two decks above, whom the ship and its crew had brought safely home through foggy seas littered with ice-floes. A number of their mess-mates had died for Britain.

Such reflections seemed not to trouble some of our party. On the contrary, as soon as we were aboard they became most jolly. What was all this about war and hardship? Was this massive breakfast impeccably served in gilded splendour normal throughout the voyage? Well, yes, sir, of course. I felt an intruder into private joy, and rapidly withdrew – somewhat shaken. I wanted only to ask the Commanding Officers of those lost ships if I could contact them later to discuss events and perhaps to record them for the future. In the circumstances the sooner I did so, obviously the better.

I stayed behind on the bridge when the ship got alongside to an emotional welcome; until, in fact, only one other person remained, clearly a civilian like myself. It was a moment to ponder, as well as to watch and draw. He asked me what I was doing with a sketch-book in my hand, and since he was a BBC reporter, he recorded a few minutes talk. I had been aboard the day the *QE II* had left Southampton, obviously I must have been to South Georgia aboard her?

The answer sadly was 'No', but I realised clearly that to complete what I had begun I must next see the Falklands, the lodestone of the early Naval actions in both the two World Wars, and now the focus of world-wide anxiety once more.

A quantity of Falkland photography and text had already appeared in Britain in thinly-filled magazines, rushed out to try to compensate for the almost total absence of live coverage, but increasingly interesting though these had become and, best of all, in moving close-up studies of people, the photographic illustrations always seemed to be timed just before things happened; or, more commonly, just afterwards. I did not need telling that this is because events in war do not oblige photographers, television teams, correspondents or anyone else. The more distant the subjects the less effective the photography seemed to become. To me, at least, it snuffed out past and future, space behind and movement beyond the border of the picture. The ships were set in concrete waves, with spray stuck in mid-air; the tramping soldier's boot would never reach the ground; the mists around the mountains were fixed in place.

Like any craftsman I could have copied these photographs, disguised maybe, in search of originality, but that would just have turned me into a sort of robot unable to research, select and reject, deprived of retrospective and creative powers. Later, this artistic resource denied to the camera but innate to any artist, was essential when I came to listen to groups of people relating their experiences; because two pairs of eyes alongside each other will sometimes see the same event quite differently and, like a visual adjudicator, I had to decide for myself what to depict in this distant trackless land with its massive seas, ice-blue, clear skies, swift and harsh changes of climate and majestic sweeping contours.

As soon, therefore, as Port Stanley had been recaptured, I sought official help from the Navy and wrote to the Admiralty to ask for a passage south. I explained what I had been doing, and what I now hoped to do. In due course I was telephoned at home to learn what places I particularly wanted to see and, fortunately, I had worked out the answers beforehand.

I was told that I would be flown by RAF VC-10 to Ascension Island, thence by Hercules to Stanley air-strip. I knew the demands on Falkland transport were intense, and that there would be no chance of seeing anything of the Islands except by helicopter, partly because there were, anyway, no roads or transport; but also the extent and siting, let alone the clearance of large areas of random minefields was still causing trouble. (The remains of livestock I saw which had come to grief on mines were to be a frequent reminder of this new fact of Falkland life). Consequently I would be flown to wherever I wanted to go, and the Army would take care of me. This was princely treatment; nobody could have been looked after with more kindness. But I was only a temporary guest. To be on duty at full alert for six months or a year often in considerable discomfort, as my hosts were, was quite a different matter.

The course and progress of this campaign had been very brief and straightforward when viewed with chart and map. The direction of advance had been unchanged from the outset of the initial landings in San Carlos Water to its victorious conclusion at Stanley. I asked, therefore, for the opportunity to inspect those two places in some detail and, in addition, to call at Fitzroy, Goose Green and Fox Bay East.

The promised view from a helicopter, almost literally the bird's eye view, is one I anticipated eagerly. I like heights anyway, and used to enjoy work aloft at sea. In a study such as this it would be invaluable to be able to hover at a given height long enough to make a drawing. It would also enable me to understand the tactical significance of San Carlos Water and the two-pronged advance of the Land Forces, laid out below me as on a relief map stretching into the distance and bordered all round by the South Atlantic. Until I actually saw this characteristic terrain I had confined my work to subjects in which it played only a minor part in composition, or did not appear at all, as in the open sea. But in this mode of transport (I had already some Fleet Air Arm experience of it in the past) one would have to be able to work quickly, as all artists can and must at times. (It was a bitterly cold day when I drew the GPMG crew who kindly posed for me for the drawing on page 57, so I lost no time. I promised them it wouldn't take long; and it didn't. Two minutes 35 seconds. They time me!)

While awaiting this long flight south and armed now with the certainty that I would shortly see things for myself, I felt able to approach other Service units which were now returning home from the Falklands almost daily. This intensely busy period put me under considerable strain. I had no conception of the sheer bulk of the research which was about to fall on me; but any fancied burdens I bore were as nothing to the satisfaction and interest of the work. Our normal domestic rural calm broken only from time to time by visiting clients, became suddenly metamorphosed by almost daily involvement with the

'...helicopters took to dropping in...'

Falkland affairs of everyone from a Lance Bombardier to the Task Force Commander Admiral Woodward himself. Assuredly, we told ourselves as the phone rang yet again, another car arrived and helicopters took to dropping in, such things might happen to other people but surely never to us.

On one day alone I was kindly shepherded by the recently-returned Lt Cdr Mike Blissett, (Senior Harrier Pilot) round four Squadrons at the Royal Naval Air Station at Yeovilton, two Helicopters (845 and 846) and two Harriers (800 and 801). I explained to each group in turn that I was powerless to do anything until they told me what they had been doing and, to prime the pump, I showed how a picture could be built up from descriptions incorporated into a succession of line sketches, each one improving slightly on the last. Or, if the drawing seemed to take a wrong turning, one could start afresh by looking at things from a different viewpoint. My first question to each group was 'What is the scene or episode which sticks in your mind?' – and as they replied and discussed I drew in front of them.

'Was it anything like this? Or more like this? Could you see that from where you were? How much light was there? Coming from where? What height were you at? What was the visibility?' etc etc.

Sometimes things went right from the outset: sometimes I had to try again. Sometimes the facts were quite clear, but they did not compose into a picture. At other times the composition was effective, but it did not really convey the required message. That evening I drove home from Yeovilton my mind full of pictures and with a sheaf of drawings and notes to be turned into further exploratory oil-sketches. As soon as these were ready I made a fresh fixture with the Squadrons to discuss what I had done.

Even as I was talking and learning I found the machinery of the Services was already restoring units, ships and men to their normal orderly pattern of movement. This smooth resumption of peacetime duties typified the quiet professionalism of the one part of the nation which really could congratulate itself on a masterly performance, but because the British are not a martial race naturally it would be unthinkable for them to say so. In any case they felt not triumph but immense relief and gratitude at this swift re-establishment of liberty under the law in place of the regime of the bullet. Even so, for my part, I had no doubt our nation's habitual apathy would soon re-assert itself. As the eighteenth century wit observed (and what he wrote holds good today)

> God and the sailor alike we adore
> But only if in danger, not before
> The danger o'er, both alike are requited
> God is forgotten and the sailor slighted.

31

5 Painting the War

Under the lively generalship of Lieut Cdr David Mowlam, their First Lieutenant, HMS *Broadsword* ship's company rounded off my first (and thoroughly-absorbing) commission for a Falkland painting by inviting me very kindly to join the ship on her way back to Plymouth from Birkenhead, and this allowed me to learn more fully the function of some of her equipment in relation to its performance in the Falklands.

She had operated actively throughout the campaign in focal areas, and though her appearance was familiar to me (she was completed in 1979 – the first of her class), I had never been aboard her or either of her sister ships *Battleaxe* and *Brilliant*; so I had much to learn. The feature which was immediately obvious from her specification was her all-missile armament and her anti-submarine role. Her defence against aircraft attack was the efficient 'Sea-Wolf' short-range missile, but since this was a point defence weapon with an outstanding performance against incoming missiles, it needed careful tactical co-ordination with the longer-range area weapon Sea-Dart, carried by the destroyers.

Broadsword sailed from the Birkenhead dockside on a still, dark, morning. The ship swung at the head of the basin and headed out past the series of silent wharves and sheds as the light grew in the sky. When we eventually reached the Mersey, it was to find a sad and empty river, and I was glad to have my 40-year-old recollection of its intense war-time activity broken into by the familiar sound of the bosun's pipe as the ship secured for sea. That past had gone for good, the future still awaited; the only reality was now, and I was a lucky part of it.

Back home again I continued my Falkland paintings with one for the Royal Navy's 846 Squadron (Sea Kings), showing their expert execution of the brilliantly-successful SAS raid on Pebble Island. Then, under their CO Lt Cdr N McMillan, they departed for their annual exercises in Norway just at the time when I needed further guidance. Instead of waiting for their return, I tried to include too much in my version of events and, alas!, how wrong I was. As soon as 846 returned I realised I must start afresh, and when Petty Officer Ashdowne (known genially as 'Splash-down') landed outside our cottage in a full-size Sea King Mk 4 bearing also a fine model of one as a present for me to guide my work, I had no excuse for error.

845 Squadron who had flown their Wessex helicopters to such effect throughout the campaign from South Georgia onwards, went a step further. In February 1985, while this book was nearing completion the squadron under their CO, Lt Cdr C de Mowbray, took me to NATO's far northern flank in Norway to study and paint their specialised style of warfare. There, the extremes of temperature, the mountains and the long Arctic night form a uniquely severe testing-ground of machines, flying skills, military deployment and, indeed, man's ability to survive. The Squadron had already showed its mastery of all these factors in the Falklands, but thanks to this imaginative commission, I was able to watch exactly how they achieved it.

In respect of the four major commissions I received from P & O, I was given every help by the Directors. Two of the Masters of their four ships were kind enough to pay me a visit to discuss their extraordinary activities, and two I visited aboard their own ships in Southampton which was, as ever, a treat for me. At a time when everyone was hard at work getting back into harness and trying to restore their ships and programmes to order, I appreciated very much their sacrifice of valuable time to help me.

The Second Battalion The Parachute Regiment asked me for large paintings of two splendid subjects, their epic capture of Goose Green and their night attack on Wireless Ridge. For the first of these I was lucky to have the benefit of Major Chris Keeble's guidance. Not once, but several times, he visited the studio, (including one occasion when his young family – lots of them – came too). To be associated so closely with such an historic battle created a particularly warm atmosphere. Progress with the work slowed when the Battalion departed to Belize for six months but even then I was able to keep painting because features like the blackened, burning gorse-line from which he controlled ably the latter stages of the action are seen often in the New Forest where I live. But I had to be taught the basis of Falkland infantry tactics; where a sniper could be sited; and where not. Also, an inescapable feature of the scene, how a casualty would be dealt with.

When I came to discuss later the successful battle for Wireless Ridge with the CO of the Battalion, Lt Col Chaundler, who planned and controlled it, he mentioned that naturally it might pose problems because it had taken place at night; but I explained that quite a number of my existing exploratory Falkland sketches involved night scenes, and that, like the Portsmouth series of Second World War paintings, these displayed plenty of colour. Indeed, in my experience, night engagements usually turned out far more colourful affairs than those by day, and I had seen a lot of them during the last war.

As he talked, and as other units approached me for paintings something very definite was forming in my mind about this series of night battles involving continuous interlocking tactics by Royal Marine Commandos, Parachutists, Guardsmen, Gunners, Seaward Naval Bombardment and aircraft.

I had noticed, when painting at Goose Green how conspicuously dark the British camouflage jackets appeared to be when compared with the Argentinian design; and how much better-adapted were the paler colours of the latter to the low levels of Falkland terrain. But it was difficult even in full daylight, to pick out anybody at all among the rock-studded mountain tops around San Carlos Water even at the short range of only ten yards (my sketch on page 76 emphasises the point), and the battle for Stanley was fought in exactly this type of terrain but in the dark.

The information from the many people I now met necessarily created more of a visual jig-saw than a coherent history of events, and in fitting together the often-unrelated pieces I travelled continually around the country as far afield as Yorkshire and Devon as well as being visited at home in Hampshire.

Watching this overall picture grow and grow, it was fascinating to learn by chance of crucial decisions taken; why certain things happened, or hadn't; how much people sometimes knew about one another's adjacent activities; (and at other times how little!). The fog of war in 1982 could be as dense as ever, but imagination, initiative and quick-thinking could still penetrate it.

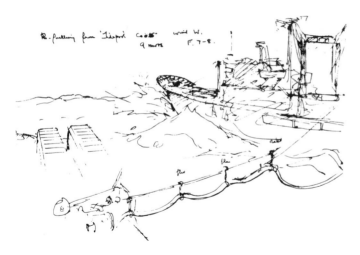

Re-fuelling from 'Tidepool' C... wind W. 9 mins F. 7-8.

Refuelling from *Tidepool*.

Naturally my queries focussed mainly on how things looked, but they also unearthed at times and by chance how they had come about. I found it very intriguing to learn how the most recent of succeeding peacetime Governments which had vacillated so persistently and how calamitously over the Falklands, had been transformed by a single, brief, ministerial phone-call into a brilliant War Cabinet, so well-able to cope with the results.

This discovery alone explained the swift Naval and other deployments, and the firm grasp and accelerating speed with which the essential supply fleet, eventually some 50 ships, was procured, converted and stored; though it also meant that throughout the long voyage south and for the duration of hostilities, there was an almost ceaseless transfer at sea of stores, fuel and personnel from one ship to another. It even extended eventually to air-drops by Hercules C-130 aircraft of the RAF of vital equipment from home and Ascension Island in mid-Atlantic. With some 900,000 items to organise, all loaded in haste, there was plenty of room for mistakes and corrections. I therefore started asking more questions about this massive preparatory operation of which so little was generally known. It took place throughout the long voyage south almost regardless of weather, and continued even in the open South Atlantic until the end. It extended to the repair of action-damage to ships while they heaved and rolled in the swell, using specialised ships and techniques designed for work among oil-rigs.

In all this the exact site and function of Ascension Island was crucial but not, unfortunately, really pictorial. Some other subjects also posed special visual problems. For example, all submarine activities, simply because they took place under water. The RAF Vulcan, which carried out the longest-range bombing raid in its history, was equally impossible to depict as it released its load on Port Stanley Air-strip at 4.23 am in the darkness of the First of May. SAS and SBS units, specialists in reconnaissance and quick-thinking, were continuously in action ashore everywhere from South Georgia to the surrender at Stanley, (and perhaps elsewhere as well), but in a manner that required a detailed knowledge of actual physical landscape, so I was unable to study them either.

Once general action was joined there arose immediately the need to transfer casualties to where they could be cared for, a role which involved helicopters

'Vertrepping'.

of all kinds in landing or hovering under fire in all conditions and round the clock. This was a continuous battlefield process, as was the dedicated work of the Field Hospital in Ajax Bay which I saw eventually in 1985.

The rigours of being a casualty change little, but the missile was certainly new to me. I had been to sea in ships fitted with Exocet, but at that time I had never seen it fired, nor had I been able to watch another ship fire it, so Exocet, Sea-Dart, Sea-Wolf, Rapier, Milan and all their self-propelling cousins were all new to me. I had everything to learn about their performance and also, in some cases, something of their detection and prior destruction.

There were other subjects such as new Army types of armour used by the Blues and Royals and specialised vehicles of which at first I knew nothing, so in order to paint them I had to be taught by their owners. I enjoy drawing and painting machinery of all kinds, also handling it or watching others do so, but there had been no opportunity or use for heavy troop-carriers or armour of the sophisticated heavy-tank type. Once ashore, the nature of the Falkland terrain took most of the warfare back to its most basic. Many of the troops covered huge distances on foot, plodding like over-laden camels across the obstacle-ridden wintery landscape; meanwhile those responsible for them were keenly aware that this process was steadily taking its toll of their ability to sustain a prolonged battle in the open.

The only fighting vehicles involved were light tanks dubbed 'combat vehicle reconnaissance and patrol' (CVRP). 'Over snow vehicles' (BV 202) conveyed troops; but both, being small and 'light-footed' proved of inestimable value and covered large mileages over the treacherous Falkland terrain, where the passage of even a single set of wheels over the fragile peat surface could render it impassable to another vehicle following behind. The guns of the Blues and Royals CVRP applied that essential extra pressure in assault; the BV 202 eased the overburdened infantry of some of their supply problems as they pounded their way the width of East Falkland over to Mount Kent, Two Sisters, Tumbledown, Mount Harriet and Wireless Ridge, where the enemy awaited them. The long line of figures, advancing into the far distance, their human shape much disguised by dress and burdens of arms, seemed symbolic of life. Nobody could turn aside, or sink down; and certainly there was no turning back.

6 Past, Present and Future

For most Service men war is long periods of tedious discomfort interspersed with flashes of violent action almost too sudden to grasp. Afterwards the first things that get remembered are, naturally, the lucky escapes, the pathos and the heroics; later, sometimes, what made people laugh. I am not a cartoonist and, even if I had been I cannot think how to do justice to the Landing Force involved in matters nautical.

When asked to bear a hand to paint the newly-fitted acreage of helicopter flight deck on their troopship, to shorten the time needed for this mammoth task, the soldiers up-ended drums of paint and waded in with brooms, to finish the whole job in minutes instead of the hours (or even days) which it might normally have taken; and when the Parachutists were equipped with expensive lifejackets for their first-ever assault by landing-craft instead of parachute-descent, they remained true to their training when they got ashore, ie above all to conceal evidence of their arrival. They certainly did leave the lifejackets, as directed, on the shore to be collected and brought back; but first they buried them, as they would their parachutes, so creating dozens of little molehills.

Perhaps the most candid illustration of this extraordinary war was the Merchant Service Captain who demurred when he learned that his ship was due to enter the battle zone of Falkland Sound the following morning. Despite the long voyage south and the steady build-up of tension, nothing could shake his sturdy sense of duty towards his ship and crew. 'I don't think I can do that' said he. 'I think I'll have to ring up my owners first.' But, on being satisfied that he was now part of the Navy and battle was, indeed, about the commence, he, and his ship, and his crew, took their station in the battle-line with the greatest resolve and distinction. As the Chinese say – 'It is those who do not delight in war who win'.

Within weeks of my return from the Falklands I had gathered 25 of the little exploratory sketches which seemed to cover the widest spectrum, and exhibited them in framed groups in London. Beneath each sketch was a handwritten note about its subject, rather like the contents of a sketch-book. The whole set was then invited for further exhibition by the Armed Forces Art Society, and finally bought by the Fleet Air Arm Museum at Yeovilton, whose Director, Commander DCB White, was at that time assembling varied features for a permanent Falkland Display in the Mountbatten Memorial Hall. In due course this was opened by His Royal Highness Prince Andrew who had flown as a Sea-King Pilot in the South Atlantic, so continuing the long tradition of active service by members of the Royal Family.

The display was a well-timed enterprise which was full of interest, and I was very proud to be involved in it. The wonderful help I had been given by everyone overrode my natural reserve of character. (It even overcame my reluctance in writing this personal Introduction to what I saw as essentially a record of Active Service in paintings). Thus I had called upon friends old and new without hesitation to help me, and so entered on a phase of intense and very happy activity when many people of my age are long on the shelf.

I have always relished new experiences (to me that is what Art is about), and even pot-holing, years ago, to help me illustrate a book, and which scared me thoroughly, I would not have missed. Now my contact with the spring-heeled Parachutists and my inquisitive nature made me want to sample a jump. 'Oh, that's no trouble', they said. 'We'll fix it. People come to us regularly for a short course. You'll like it.'

Soon afterwards I was talking to one of the 'Jungly' Fleet Air Arm Squadrons, and mentioned the Parachutist's invitation, and my intention to take it up as soon as I had the opportunity. They looked at my grey head a little thoughtfully, and then said kindly that it might be wiser to come to them; because I might find land rather hard and break something. They offered to drop me in the sea, which was softer (though, of course, I might get under my parachute and drown). I had received such grand help and encouragement from their Commanding Officer at RNAS Yeovilton, Captain P Williams, CBE, RN, that I felt it incumbent not to drown without giving him due notice, at which he wrote me a delightfully paternal letter, admonishing me sternly against any such madness while within his command, whatever antics I might get up to with the Parachutists.

So I reach the end of my modest odyssey, or rather the part of it that has happened so far; because it seems it is not yet ended. I have more people to meet who have new things to teach me by air, land and sea. We shall talk, and I shall draw as we do so. Then I shall wave them goodbye as they drive away from my cottage through the woods, or depart skywards, and I shall return to my studio with its ship and aircraft models and momentos of Service life to think about where to start, how soon they may come again to see me, or where I am to join them. At sea? In Norway? Germany? In the Falklands again? Besides, there is still that parachute jump to do ...

The Falklands Paintings

1 *COLOUR*

HMS Hermes, Task Force Flagship

(Exploratory oil sketch 16″×10″, property of Fleet Air Arm Museum)

Built in 1959, HMS *Hermes* is primarily an anti-submarine (A/S) carrier, equipped to operate anti-submarine Sea-King Helicopters; but she has a secondary role as a Commando carrier when so-called 'Jungly' Sea-Kings can land troops. Both *Hermes* and *Invincible*, in their role of mobile airfields for the 35 Harriers, were indispensable for the repossession of the Falklands. The loss or immobilisation of either ship from submarine or air attack would almost certainly have ended the operation.

To reduce these risks, the Battle Group generally stayed as far to the East as was consistent with the requirement to maintain adequate Sea Harrier Combat Air Patrols over forces inshore. At night, when the threat of Argentinian air attack diminished markedly, the carriers went forward for a variety of tasks of which the main ones were Special Reconnaissance force insertion by Sea-King Mk 4 from *Hermes*, the raid on Pebble Island airstrip from *Hermes* and a series of forays by *Invincible* in an attempt to find the Argentinian Hercules Supply Aircraft.

Until the Landing Force was ashore, all progress was a Naval responsibility directed from *Hermes*,

controlling an invisible battle over islands occupied by an enemy of unknown strength. All resources came from 8000 miles away which ruled out any quick replacement of losses, no matter how urgently needed.

Once the Landing Force was safely established, its power to advance hinged on the build-up of supplies from the floating arsenal sited far out in the South Atlantic, of which *Hermes* was the controlling influence and, naturally, a vital target for the enemy.

HMS *Hermes* flew the Flag of Rear-Admiral John Woodward, Commander of the Task Force throughout the war. Her Commanding Officer was Captain LE Middleton and that of HMS *Invincible* was Captain JJ Black.

2

South Georgia Rescue – 21 April 1982

(Exploratory oil sketch 16″×10″, property of Fleet Air Arm Museum)

To recover South Georgia from the Argentinians, three ships sailed south from Ascension; 180 men of M Company 42 Commando Royal Marines, 22 SAS and 148 Commando Forward Observation Battery, RA were aboard HMS *Antrim*, HMS *Endurance* and RFA *Tidespring*.

On 21 April two of the ships stood off about 200 miles, while *Antrim* closed to about 10 miles from the coast in very rough weather and snow-showers, to try to land patrols.

At their first attempt the two Wessex helicopters were unable to see to land on the Fortuna glacier, and had to return to the ship.

At 10 am the patrols were landed successfully, but very soon the weather shut down so savagely that soon they had to be withdrawn hastily before the men died of exposure in the 100 mph blizzard at sub-zero temperatures.

The first rescue attempt failed because the aircraft could not sight the patrols. The second was a double disaster. One Wessex crashed on take-off because of white-out conditions. A second, sent to recover everyone, also crashed on take-off due to the same weather conditions. This left 17 men on the glacier, and one remaining Wessex capable of lifting only five men. The pilot, Lt Cdr Stanley, successfully lifted everyone, and on reaching *Antrim* with his overladen plane, he dispensed with normal procedures to make sure of landing on the heaving, rolling ship to ensure the survival of his valuable freight.

The 'white-out' conditions which occur in such latitudes are unlike anything normally experienced in Britain. They are likely to cause pilot-disorientation due to the sudden loss of visual references just as the pilot is taking off or landing.

This narrow escape from initial disaster had a crucial effect, for it allowed the operation to develop, and to end in success, when nothing but success was enough.

'FEARLESS' GOING SOUTH

3 COLOUR
Replenishment at Sea (RAS)
(Exploratory sketch 16″×10″, By kind permission of Vice-Admiral Sir John Woodward, KCB)

On the success of self-supporting abilities of the Task Force afloat rested that of the Landing Force ashore. To transfer stores, fuel and equipment between ships at sea they must steam on parallel courses at exactly the same speed while using specially designed derricks and hoses, cargo-nets, and other means. Ideally this takes place between two ships only, in daylight in calm seas. In war, 845 Squadron (Wessex 5 Helicopters, CO Lieutenant-Commander R Warden) described a night on their way South when HMS *Invincible*, RFA *Tidepool*, HMS *Glasgow* and RFA *Stromness* were all engaged at night in a four-ship RAS with ships blacked out, the helicopter landings only dimly lit, and masthead lights showing.

To maintain the Fleet in the war zone the supply fleet totalled eventually some fifty ships, in order to supply and where necessary repair at sea, about another fifty; all of this via Ascension Island and activities in the open sea.

The idea that an airfield can exist at sea is difficult to convey beyond the moment when an aircraft takes off or lands. This little sketch was in response to discussions with the Task Force Commander about the actual work, carried out on windswept decks in heavy seas, which alone makes operations possible.

4

FORTUNA GLACIER 21/4/82   DAVID COBB

4
HMS Fearless 'Crossdecking' en route South – 23–28 April 1982
(Exploratory oil sketch 16″×10″, property of Fleet Air Arm Museum)

'...ships were pitching 15° and rolling 30°...'

Before the Task Force sailed there was no agreed plan on how the Falklands were to be repossessed; so there was no pre-prepared scheme of loading for the many ships needed for the job. Supplies and stores, ammunition and armaments were therefore shipped off on an ad hoc basis, and the many resulting flaws and imbalances were sorted out on the way by procedures known as 'crossdecking' and 'vertrepping' (vertical replenishment, ie transfers by air).

This process is highly skilled and the Royal Navy excels in it. In suitable weather conditions it is carried out by direct transfer of pallets slung on a jackstay held taut between two ships as they steam along on parallel courses, some fifty to a hundred feet apart. This is called RAS (replenishment at sea), but when the sea conditions or other factors do not allow of this method, helicopters alone are used.

846 Squadron (Sea King Mk IV) described to me landing and taking off, crossdecking with *Fearless* and other ships, when they were 'pitching 15 degrees and rolling 30 degrees', which is what my exploratory sketch shows. To add to the difficulties, the helicopter decks were already cluttered with ammunition boxes, containers and other helicopters which were 'taking passage', Scout and Gazelle, etc on deck. Between

23–28 April the Squadron had to shift supplies and stores between *Canberra*, HMS *Fearless*, HMS *Intrepid*, *Norland*, the four LSLs, *Elk* and RFA *Fort Toronto*.

The Commanding Officer of HMS *Fearless*, Captain ESJ Larken, RN, kindly advised me that in his opinion the sea conditions I had shown originally were too severe and I therefore moderated them to conform with his advice.

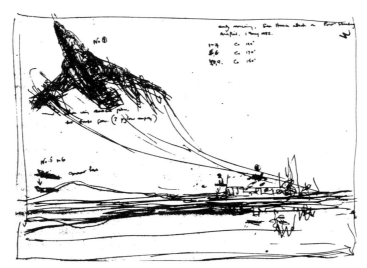

5

Harriers Attack Port Stanley Airstrip
– 1 May 1982

(Exploratory oil sketch 16″×10″, property of Fleet Air Arm Museum)

The runway at Port Stanley had already been attacked by the RAF Vulcan during the early morning hours of 1 May. At daybreak the same day, nine Sea Harriers of 800 and 899 Squadrons made a fresh low-level attack using a mix of 1000lb tossed and retarded tail-bombs and cluster-bombs. Cluster-bombs contain a number of charges which scatter under spring-loading, and form an explosive carpet under the path of the aircraft.

To distract the defences the first four aircraft approached on a course of 190° and tossed their 1000lb bombs from a range of three miles. The next two attacked with cluster bombs on a course of 170° and the last three on 150° again with cluster bombs, all within a few seconds of each other. No aircraft was lost, and the attack was successful, leaving Argentinian aircraft and installations on fire on the airfield.

Visible behind the airfield on the left is Mount Low; to seaward; rain clouds were along the horizon; and on the airfield itself and cluster bombs sparkled as they exploded. Under the Harrier, as it pulls up, the under-wing tanks are still in place but, with the bombs gone, three pylons are empty.

6

Bombardment of Port Stanley Airstrip
– 1 May 1982

(Oil painting 30″×18″, commissioned by the Royal Naval Museum, Portsmouth)

Following the air-strike at dawn by the Harriers on the airstrip, a bombarding force of HM Ships *Alacrity* (foreground), *Arrow* and *Glamorgan* closed the land from the southward and opened fire at a range of about eight miles on the already-burning airfield.

At first the gunfire was directed from *Alacrity*'s Lynx, until it was hit by anti-aircraft fire and had to return to the ship. The visual appearance of the combined gunfire as it showed on the radar screen was 'like a waterfall ... with all the bricks going north from the four guns ...' (Lt Cdr de Mowbray). *Arrow*'s Lynx then took over fire control.

Soon after the bombardment had begun the Argentinian Air Force responded with an air attack by four Mirages, one of which was destroyed by Argentinian anti-aircraft fire from the shore, falling into the sea between the shore and the ships. The remaining Mirages attacked the ships with bombs and rockets, causing minor damage but no direct hits.

The above scene and details were the result of help kindly provided by the nearest, ie most western, of the ships involved (HMS *Alacrity* CO Cdr CJS Craig and Lt Cdr CJ de Mowbray) and by Lt Col KRH Eve, RA, CO Naval Gunfire Support in the Falklands.

Queen Elizabeth II Sails from Southampton – 12 May 1982

(Exploratory oil sketch 16″×10″, property of Commander D Joel, RN)

At 1600 on 12 May, with some 3000 men of Scots and Welsh Guards and Gurkhas embarked, the ship sailed for the South Atlantic. To prepare her for her new role she had been fitted fore and aft with a total of some 9000 square feet of helicopter decks; also a full set of satellite navigation and communication equipment, all within nine days of cancelling her planned cruises and dis-

embarking her 1750 passengers; cancelling also the bookings of 18000 others.

The work to be done alongside at Southampton (which included fitting her for refuelling at sea) had involved berthing the ship heading upstream; so, after leaving the quay under the care of eight tugs on a brilliant sunny afternoon, she moved slowly up-river to where she could be swung. Then she returned past the quays, on her way seaward. She was seen off by two bands which had been playing in front of a huge crowd of relatives, well-wishers and dignitaries, many from long distances. All had come to see her sail.

I had made my first studies from ashore in the morning, high on the Control Tower; but after going aboard to continue drawing, I concluded that this would also be the best vantage point from which to paint the ship's departure. I returned there shortly before sailing time. There was a strong-to-gale ESE wind, and clouds of dust, but I managed to paint-in the composition of the scene, ready for when the ship moved into the centre of it, which she duly did. The grains of sand and other flying debris which stuck to the painting as I worked are there for ever – a physical reminder of that day.

8 COLOUR

RAF Hercules 'Take-Off At Dawn' from Wideawake Airstrip, Ascension Island

(Exploratory oil sketch 16″ × 10″, property of 70 Squadron RAF)

Volcanic Ascension Island, some five miles across, has no harbour and lies about 600 miles south of the Equator – 1000 miles from land, just over half the 8000 miles distance between UK and the Falklands. Formerly the site for a World War II staging airstrip, in the 1960s, it became a Satellite Communications Centre and its airfield was expanded. In April/May of 1982 that airfield handled more air traffic daily than Idlewild Airport in the USA.

Much of this traffic, crucial to the southward progress of the British Task Force, comprised RAF Hercules transport aircraft, ferrying urgently-needed specialist equipment and key personnel. To fit them for the increasingly long ranges they had to cover, in-flight refuelling (from Victors and other Hercules) was quick designed, fitted and brought into use. This procedure allowed Hercules to reach the Falklands zone during the conflict and enabled the so-called 'Airbridge' between Ascension and Stanley to start the moment the

Islands were recaptured. This subsequent service was an essential factor in manning and building-up the British military hold. Between 1982–85 flying hours totalled 19,356; nautical miles 6,301, 900; freight 21,250,000lb; passengers 41,650, spread over 935 round flights. It forms a remarkable record. The Hercules was designed for a variety of specialist military roles but never as a long-range passenger-carrying aircraft. However, its cavernous hold, jammed full with men and women, regardless of Service or occupation, and stacked with stretcher-cases and cargo, formed a unique travel experience. The monotony of cramped, noisy and very long flights of about 13 hours' duration was relieved by everyone's determination, particularly that of the crew, to make the best of things for everyone else. The sharpest test was when, as sometimes happened, the aircraft reached the Falklands only to be turned back to Ascension because atrocious weather conditions intervened to prevent landing.

Wing-Commander BP Nicolle, OC 70 Squadron (Hercules) kindly provided the above figures, and Flt Lt Pembrey and his crew showed how it was done in May 1985 aboard Flight No ASCOT 8 189, the very last passenger 'Airbridge'.

9 COLOUR

The Pebble Island Raid – 15 May 1982

(Oil painting 26″ × 18″ entitled 'PEBBLE ISLAND EXTRACTION' in memory of Cpl (AGMN) DOC Love, DSC, RM 846 Squadron)

The Argentinian Air Force used Pebble Island, 25 miles NW of Falkland Sound, as an airfield from which to fly their ground-attack Pucaras. These were an obvious threat to the planned landings in San Carlos Water, so

the SAS mounted a raid to put them out of action.

Two Mk IV Sea-Kings of 846 Squadron (CO Lt Commander S Thornewill) dropped the raiding party on the south side of Pebble Island on the night of 14 May. Aided by earlier reconnaissance they put out of action 11 aircraft on the ground, set fire to fuel store (visible burning in the distance) and withdrew in good order to where the two Sea-Kings landed on time to pick them up. This raid was a total success of far-reaching consequence, and the scene shows the two aircraft coming in low over the shore in quarter-line, the leader turning to port and the second one banking as it turns to keep station.

A week later, during night crossdecking operations at sea, one of the two Sea-Kings, with its crew and a party of SAS aboard, was tragically lost, probably by hitting sea-birds and losing power. The Squadron and relatives of those who died commissioned the painting as a memorial to the sad event, and it hangs in the Fleet Air Arm Museum at the Royal Naval Air Station, Yeovilton, where 846 Squadron is based.

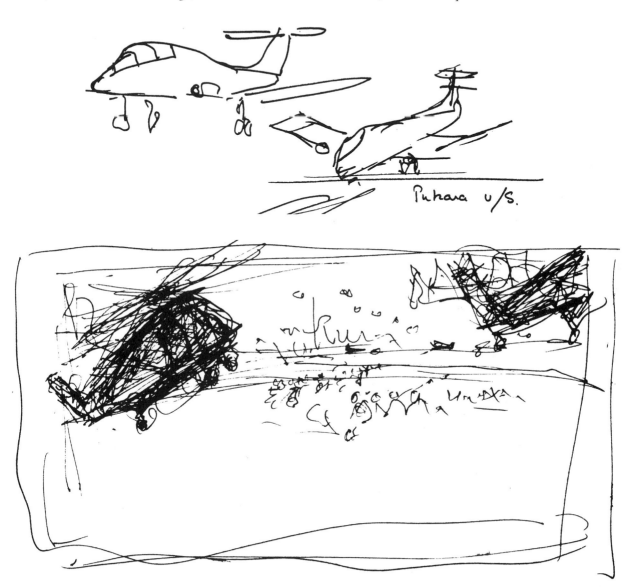

San Carlos Water from Fanning Head
– 21 May 1982

Ships on the Naval Gunfire Support 'Gun Line'
(Exploratory oil sketch 16″×10″ property of Lt Col KRH Eve, RA. Preparatory to 26″×18″ painting commissioned by 148 (Meiktala) Commando Forward Observation Battery, RA)

The gun-power of nearby ships has always been, and still is, a potent factor when troops are making a landing against opposition. The direction and control of these guns is a specialised function shared today between ships and the versatile Naval Gunfire Forward Observers of the Commando Regiment, Royal Artillery, who land with the troops, or are prepositioned before the landing. They may operate from the air by parachute or helicopters; from the sea from fast inflatable dinghies or canoes, or independently on their own. They are at home in all three elements, which made their contribution in the Falklands terrain uniquely effective, and where they were operating for three weeks before the landing at San Carlos. They directed 63 bombardments firing 8000

rounds of 4.5in shell everywhere from Grytviken to the final surrender at Stanley. Fourteen Royal Naval ships came into the bombarding gun line which they controlled, of which three were sunk and nine damaged.

The first requirement at San Carlos was for HMS *Antrim* to neutralise the Argentinian defences at Fanning Head which covers the entrance to Falkland Sound. These defences lay just out of sight below the scene depicted and, after prior location by helicopter patrol in the dark, *Antrim*'s gunfire put it out of action while the fleet moved uninterrupted into Falkland Sound and anchored.

As daylight grew the retreating enemy were rounded up by the Special Boat Service patrol which had been put ashore before the first wave of the landings, and who are visible with the Forward Observation Team under Capt McManners, RA, in the foreground of the sketch.

I am indebted to Lt Col KRH Eve, RA for the data and background above, which I was able to assemble into a sketch from his notes made at the time, and my own airborne sketches, made from HMS *Glasgow*'s Lynx.

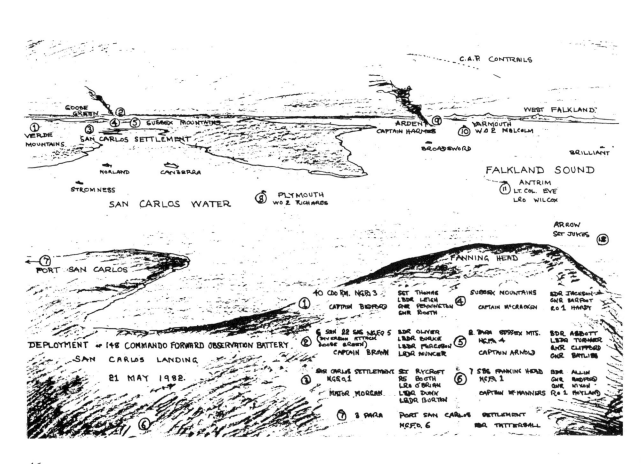

11 COLOUR
The Landing at Green Beach, Port San Carlos Settlement – 21 May 1982
The Third Battalion The Parachute Regiment
(Lt Col Hew Pike, MBE)
The Blues and Royals B Troop of CVRTs
(Lt Mark Coreth)

(*Exploratory oil sketch 16″×10″, property of Fleet Air Arm Museum.*
Oil Painting 26″×18″, commissioned by The Blues and Royals)

The Third Battalion The Parachute Regiment and one troop of 2 Scimitars, 2 Scorpions and a Samson of The Blues and Royals landed from the LCUs of HMS *Fearless* at Sand Bay, 1½ miles to the west of Port San Carlos Settlement, to take control of the area. To quote the CO of the Parachutists in a letter to me – 'it was a particularly beautiful morning'.

3 Para, like every other formation which crossed East Falkland in the days to come, were soon to create their own special legends and win their own battle honours, including a VC, around the crest of Mount Longdon.

The CVRTs of The Blues and Royals (combat vehicles reconnaissance and patrol) and their crews proved effective far beyond all expectations on the formidable Falkland terrain. Each covered some 300 miles of the roughest going imaginable, and apart from one damaged by a mine, all were in at the finish on Tumbledown and Wireless Ridge, exercising their extra weight of fire-power at the right place and time.

I was very kindly taught something of CRVTs by The Blues and Royals at Combermere Barracks, Windsor, and of their service in the Falklands by Captain Roger Field and Lieutenant Mark Coreth (whose Troop appears above).

The scene is looking towards Fanning Head from the vicinity of the Port San Carlos Settlement Airstrip where I landed.

12

1

3

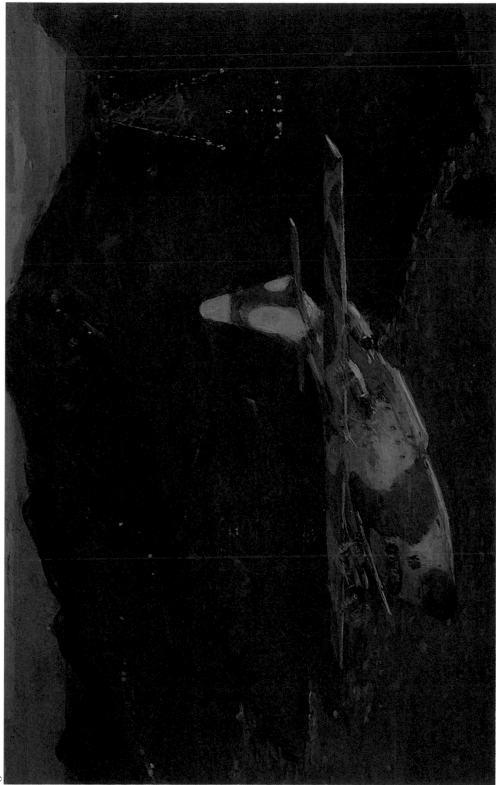

11

SAN CARLOS 21-24 MAY   David Cobb

15

19

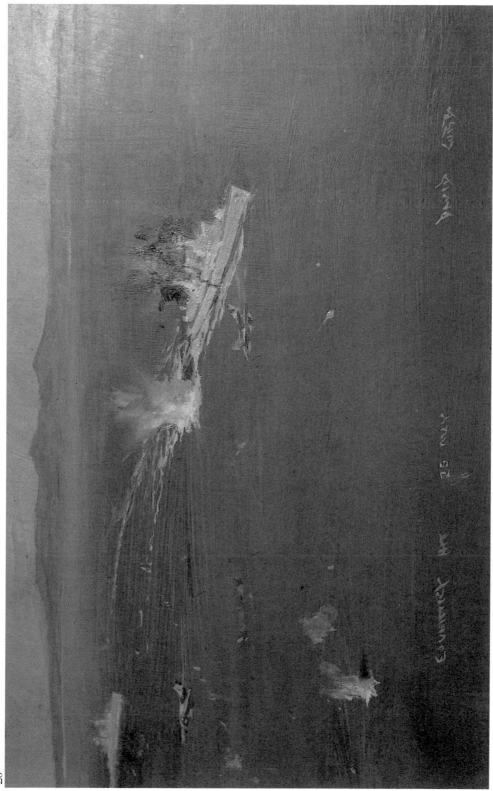

21

39

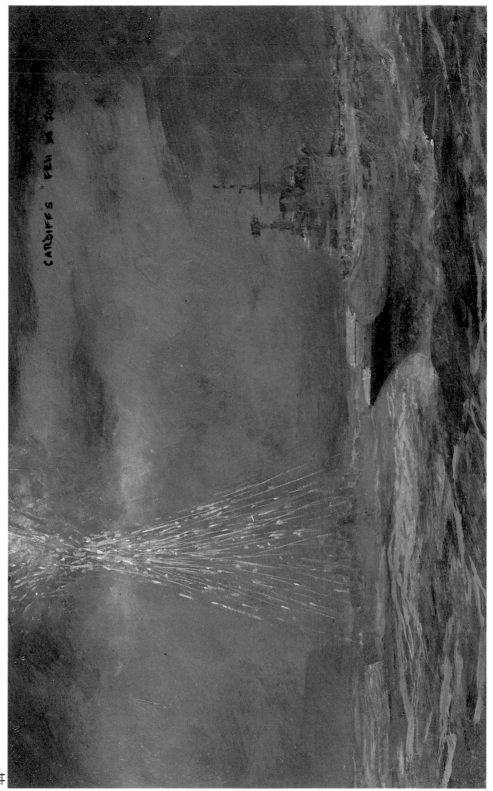

CARDIFF'S "FEN" &c Zee

44

12

Canberra Anchored in San Carlos
– 21 May 1982
(*Exploratory oil sketch 16″ × 10″, property of Fleet Air Arm Museum.*
Oil painting 30″×24″, commissioned by P & O Steamship Company)

The Task Force landing fleet had anchored first in darkness, out in Falkland Sound, to disembark the first wave of troops. As dawn broke *Canberra, Norland,* plus the Naval Assault Ships and Fleet Auxiliaries entered San Carlos Water to continue the landings. The first enemy reaction to affect *Canberra* came at 0845 when a low-flying reconnaissance aircraft rounded Fanning Head from the north, first attacking HMS *Argonaut* (visible in the distance) with rocket-fire, before turning south towards *Canberra* and *Norland*.

Canberra opened fire with machine guns and

Blowpipe, and the plane was finally hit by a frigate's 4.5 gun and destroyed.

The air-attacks intensified greatly during the day, with successive flights of Mirage and Skyhawks flying low over the fleet. Their attacks were concentrated mainly on the warships stationed out in Falkland Sound of which they sank one, HMS *Ardent*, badly damaged another and hit three more with bombs which failed to explode.

The threat to *Canberra* was obvious and acute, but she remained unharmed, and continued unloading at speed until 2242 when she weighed anchor and headed seawards out of Falkland Sound.

The first sketches I composed aboard *Canberra* with the help of her master, Captain DJ Scott Masson, and the painting was greatly helped by Captain CPO Burne, Royal Navy, who served aboard her as Naval Liaison Officer throughout her service.

13 COLOUR

The Argentinian Air Force over San Carlos
(*Exploratory oil sketch 16″ × 10″, property of Fleet Air Arm Museum*)

The odds between the two opposing air-forces over the Falklands was hard to assess beforehand. On paper the Argentinians had a big superiority in numbers, but all their bases were some 400 miles away on the mainland, and their pilots were unaccustomed to operating over the sea. Their 68 American Skyhawks were 20 years old, and their 44 Mirages though supersonic at high altitudes, were not as agile as the Harrier.

The attackers well-founded respect for the British missile systems caused them to adopt a low-level approach to the islands, right down on the sea-surface, and a ground-hugging flight-path once over the land. This profile left them little or no time as they topped the hills and dived on San Carlos Water to recover for

their bombing run; but despite these limitations the pilots flew resolutely. Once free of their bombs the pilots' evasive action threw the planes violently about in the sky, where they were pursued by varied missiles from the ships and Rapier sites, as well as by small-arms fire from the troops on shore.

The Sea Harrier's high rate of hitting was due to the AIM 9L Sidewinder missile's all-aspect capability to engage a target whether it be stern-on, or a crossing target. Engagement took place away from the anchorage beyond the range of own forces weapon systems.

If the Argentinians had risked a saturation attack on the ships in San Carlos Water on the first day of the landings, it seems almost certain that they could have caused much damage, but that was a risk that the British accepted, and taking such risks is an inescapable part of war.

14 COLOUR

HM Ships Antelope and Broadsword – 23 May 1982
(*Exploratory oil sketch 16″×10″, property of Fleet Air Arm Museum*)

Following the successful landings on 21 May, as many supply ships as possible were withdrawn seawards to avoid air attacks, and the protective 'gun-line' of warships could be brought into the north end of San Carlos Water from Falkland Sound.

Here HMS *Antelope* brought down one Skyhawk; but she was hit by a bomb from another. The plane then collided with her mast, and disintegrated into what Commanding Officer (Commander N J Tobin) described to me as 'a ball of flame'. Pieces of the aircraft flew a long way, some nearly reaching HMS *Broadsword* beyond.

Antelope was then hit by a second bomb from a Skyhawk which lodged beneath the bridge but, like the first, it failed to explode. Meanwhile, the ship was at risk until these had been defused. To allow this attempt to be made in a less-exposed position (for the ship's company and the engine room staff had had to come on deck) *Antelope* moved first to a position further into San Carlos Water, and then anchored.

Two NCOs from the Royal Engineers embarked to try to defuse the first of the bombs, but in the process it detonated, killing one RE and badly injuring the other. The resulting blast severed essential power and fire-fighting services, and the ship had to be abandoned shortly afterwards.

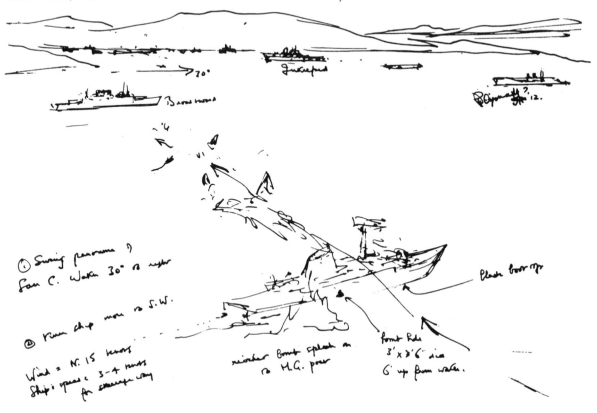

15 *COLOUR*
Norland Near-Missed – 24 May 1982
(Oil painting 30″×24″, commissioned by P & O Steamship Company.
Exploratory oil sketch 16″×10″, property of Fleet Air Arm Museum)

When *Norland* entered San Carlos Water, she had replaced her normal Hull-Rotterdam passengers with the men of the 2nd Battalion, The Parachute Regiment, to be the first ship to enter San Carlos Water at daybreak on 21 May 1982.

Within hours the Argentinian Air Force began a series of determined, low-level attacks upon the British ships, concentrating at first upon the Naval defenders of which, in the end, they sank three, and damaged a number of others.

Norland was anchored off Doctor's Point, towards the northern end of the anchorage, when on 24 May she came nearest to being hit when two bombs straddled her. These attacks, being at low level, gave the bombs a horizontal trajectory on release. The resulting explosions consequently were at shallow depth, causing a dispersed spray, rather than the vertical column of water associated with high-level bombing.

The ship was shaken, but unharmed. She continued to serve very actively; next by helping *Canberra* to ferry 5 Brigade from the *QE II* at Grytviken, in S Georgia. After the surrender she embarked a total of 2047 Argentinian prisoners-of-war (and two dogs) for repatriation.

The Master of *Norland* was Captain John Ellerby from whom I learned the very notable contribution of his ship to the success of the operations.

San Carlos Water – 24 May 1982

(Oil painting 60″ × 48″, commissioned by the Army and Navy Club, Pall Mall, London. The preliminary 40″ × 26″ oil study was purchased by the Royal Naval Museum, Portsmouth – see Frontispiece)

The Army and Navy Club wished to commemorate in a single large work the maximum number of units and ships which played a part in the Falklands campaign. The key to the successful outcome was the landing in San Carlos Water, which is entered past Fanning Head to the North, and around which the three major landings were made at Ajax Bay (West), San Carlos Settlement (East) and Port San Carlos Settlement (North-East).

To organise this very large concept I started with a drawing based on hovering the HMS *Glasgow*'s Lynx on the morning of 13 October 1982, and on walking the foreshores of Blue Beach 1 and 2 (foreground) and Little Rincon airstrip.

Fanning Head is some nine miles distant from the observer, so the individual man, where he is visible at all in such a huge scene, is minute. But very many were out of sight, eg 3 Para and 42 Commando Royal Marines were over the brow of the ridge to the right, at Port San Carlos; 45 Commando Royal Marines were at Ajax Bay,

out of sight to the left; 2 Para were behind the observer, reached by the foreground track to the right of the scene, which led to their hill-top defence position on Sussex Mountains.

In the long harbour lay a number of ships anchored, urgently unloading the supplies needed by the Landing Force before it could start its advance across the island to Stanley. Among them were several warships repairing damage inflicted by the Argentinian Air Force. In the centre, beneath a pail of smoke, there projected above the surface the bows of the sunken Type 21 Frigate HMS *Antelope*, one of three ships of the Royal Navy lost in the defence of this anchorage. Smoke from a crashed enemy aircraft rises from West Falkland.

On the surrounding mountain-tops there were situated a number of anti-aircraft missile defence units of the Royal Artillery, and all along the hillsides and to and fro, there worked a tireless shuttle service of helicopters. A useful addition to the Landing Forces' own vehicles were the powerful Falkland Island farm tractors and trailers, one of which appears in the foreground.

The officer responsible for this operation was Brigadier JHA Thompson, OBE (whose Brigade HQ was in the middle ground Blue Beach), and whose help to me in assembling these facts was invaluable.

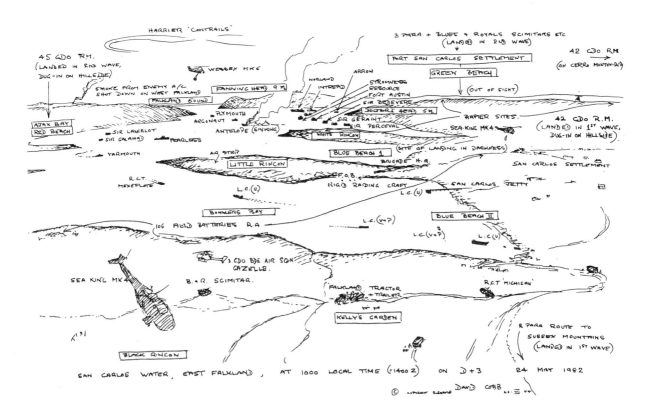

17

Ajax Bay Field Hospital Hit by Bombs – 1900/27
May 1982
(Oil sketch 20″×12″, property of the Artist)

Apart from buildings in Stanley, there is only one really large structure in the whole of the rest of the islands. This is the abandoned refrigeration plant at Ajax Bay, San Carlos Water, which was promptly commandeered by the Landing Force to serve as a Field Hospital. Conditions inside were bleak and spartan, but there was shelter from the harsh winter climate, and underfoot was a smooth dry concrete floor, both of them features rare and highly-prized in Falkland warfare. On the hillside above the plant 45 Commando, RM dug itself in.

Two make-shift operating theatres were manned round the clock by 4 Para and Naval Surgeons, 3 anaesthetists and 100 nurses and orderlies. All except 2 (gravely injured) casualties who reached Ajax Bay alive also left it safely for *Canberra* or the hospital ship *Uganda*. To achieve this record the surgeons carried out 202 major operations, more than one-third of them on Argentinians, as well as 100 carried out elsewhere on the islands.

Work continued regardless of Argentinian air attacks including that at 1900 on 27 May, when a Skyhawk (later shot down by a Rapier missile) dropped four 1000lb

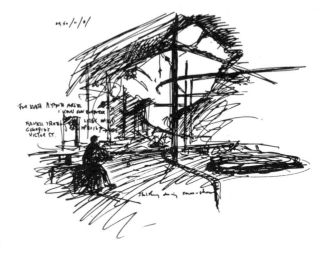

bombs on the plant. One bomb exploded killing 5 men at the southern end of the building; 2 lodged unexploded in its structure and one passed right through to land on open ground outside.

At the suggestion of Lt Col P Lutter, RAMC at Stanley in May 1985 I visited Ajax Bay and was subsequently briefed by Lt M Sterba, RAMC who was one of the team of Para surgeons working at the Field Hospital when it was hit.

54

18

Uganda Entering Falkland Sound
(Oil painting 30″×24″, commissioned by P & O Steamship Company. Exploratory oil sketch 16″ × 10″, property of Fleet Air Arm Museum)

The genesis of this painting was the surprise meeting between the brilliantly-lit *Uganda* as she entered Falkland Sound at night and the blacked-out *Elk*, which suddenly found ahead of her and the convoy she was in, this unidentified and unexplained ball of glowing flame on the horizon. What new type of missile might this be?

The nightly convoys (HMS *Andromeda* appears to the right of *Uganda*) got used to these meetings with *Uganda* when the ships often passed within a cable or two of one another.

Uganda's service as a hospital ship left her Master, Captain Clark, with some vivid memories, among them the giant overweight Chinook helicopter which landed successfully on her in very heavy weather, and the great swell which rolled up endlessly from the direction of Cape Horn. The statistics are impressive. Converted to a hospital ship at Gibraltar in 67 hours; 1044 helicopter landings, carrying 3111 persons. 903 surgical operations. 730 casualties treated (150 Argentinians); 26,150 miles steam.

19 COLOUR

Baltic Ferry and Mexeflote in San Carlos Water

(Exploratory oil sketch 16"×10", property of Fleet Air Arm Museum)

Baltic Ferry and *Nordic Ferry* normally operated on North Sea crossings, carrying the largest of roll-on roll-off container vehicles. Their stern ramps needed supplementary 'wedges' to connect them to simple jetties or pontoons, and these and other modifications to fit them for military and naval Falkland service took only four days in Portsmouth Dockyard. This included strengthening the upper deck to accept the landing impact of Sea-King helicopters. Thereafter both ships loaded at Southampton with a wide range of military vehicles, equipment and combat supplies.

In San Carlos Water their freight could now be discharged by helicopters operating from the upper deck, and by Mexeflote self-propelled rafts operating from the stern ramp. These were able to handle the heaviest items, ferrying them to the shore.

The Mexeflote is the modern use of the ancient military pontoon of history. The rafts are made up from easily-connected, modular cells of varying functions. The standard raft is driven by two large diesel outboard engines and has a pay-load of 120 tons. The bow cells have a hydraulically-operated ramp which can adjust to the angle of the beach or hard. (Complete Mexeflote rafts can be carried by the RFA specialised LSLs of the *Sir Launcelot* class, or in sections aboard normal freighters).

Mexeflote was able to discharge cargo onto Falkland beaches or improvised hards from the stern ramps of all Ro-Ro ferries that were taken up from trade. In deep and unprotected water it proved itself able to operate in sea states far exceeding those for which it had been designed (eg 6 foot waves operational, 12 foot survival), and overall proved itself an outstanding success. I examined Blue Beach at San Carlos, and a hard at Port Stanley which was in use at the time by Mexeflote, but Major RHG Barton, MBE, RCT, late of Falklands, kindly provided details of how the Royal Corps of Transport operated this particular technique.

20 COLOUR

HMS Coventry Hit – 25 May 1982

(Exploratory oil sketch 16"×10", property of Fleet Air Arm Museum)

To counter Argentinian air attacks and give maximum early warning of their approach to the ships anchored in San Carlos Water, HMS *Coventry* (Type 42 destroyer) and HMS *Broadsword* (Type 22 frigate) were stationed at sea some 25 miles north-west of the anchorage where *Coventry*'s Sea Dart and radar could operate to best advantage. *Broadsword* carried Sea-Wolf close-range air-defence missiles (which *Coventry* lacked), and by 'goal-keeping' close to *Coventry* she could expect to give cover to both *Coventry* and herself.

On the 25 May HMS *Coventry* destroyed three aircraft with Sea-Dart missiles, but later that same day she was overwhelmed by a determined attack from four fighter bombers coming from the direction of the islands. One of the aircraft hit *Coventry* with three 1000lb bombs which exploded deep inside the hull. There was no hope of being able to save the ship, and later that afternoon she sank after a brilliant rescue operation by helicopters from the islands, from ships in San Carlos and *Broadsword* herself. More than 270 men were saved but, tragically, 19 of her company were killed.

The final layout of this preliminary sketch was dictated by the distance between the aircraft and the ship at the moment when the bombs exploded. If *Coventry* herself was a prominent foreground feature of the sketch, the aircraft would have been mere dots in the distance. The final solution shown is therefore a compromise with truth, for the two aircraft would have been even further from *Coventry* at the moment shown.

Coventry's Commanding Officer, Captain D Hart-Dyke, MVO, kindly helped me to produce this version of the incident.

21 COLOUR

Loss of HMS Coventry off The Falklands – 25 May 1982

(Oil painting 26"×18", commissioned by HMS Broadsword)

This painting was commissioned by the ship's company of HMS *Broadsword*, and it hangs in the main passageway on board.

The pictorial features were comparatively straightforward, but to balance appropriately the aspects of pathos and courage was a delicate matter. *Broadsword*, and the helicopters which came hurrying out from the islands, mounted a very fine operation. Both rescuers and rescued conducted themselves with great distinction. The painting had to pay tribute accordingly.

It will be noted that *Broadsword* herself had not

escaped damaged from the same air-attack, when a bomb ricocheted up through the ship's side from the sea, wrecked the Lynx on the helicopter flight deck, and so prevented the rescue helicopters from landing there as they normally would.

I was helped greatly by *Broadsword*'s First Lieutenant, Lt Cdr D Mowlam, and her Squadron Weapon Engineer Officer, Commander J Castle.

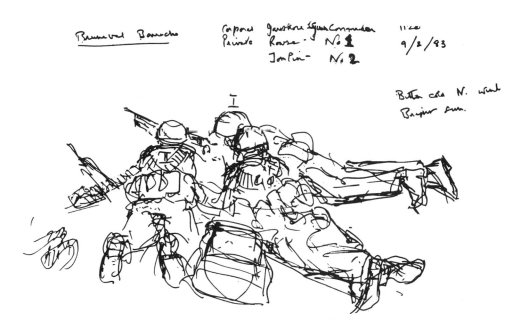

22 COLOUR

Goose Green – 28 May 1982

(Exploratory oil sketch 16″ × 10″, property of Fleet Air Arm Museum. Oil painting 30″ × 60″, commissioned by The Second Battalion The Parachute Regiment)

While being shown the field of battle between Darwin and Goose Green I stood on the gorse line overlooking Goose Green from which the latter stage of that epic was directed by Major Chris Keeble, following on the death of the CO Lt Col H Jones, who was awarded the VC.

By the time 2 Para had captured this position they had been fighting their way forward over ground largely devoid of cover for nearly 24 hours, with little artillery and no air support because of low visibility. Opposed to them was a series of well-sited and strongly-armed defensive positions which had to be taken one by one to allow any further advance. Daylight brought increasing casualties and stalemate except for an outflanking manoeuvre which relied on concentrating the fire-power of the Battalion and inserting a company along the shoreline for about 1000 yards on the right of the painting, out of sight to the Argentinian defenders on the skyline of the picture. This turning of the left flank of the main Argentinian positions proved the key to the battle. It ended by 2 Para forcing the defenders into a perimeter inside Goose Green, when the enemy's will to fight was finally broken by the added intervention of Harrier close air-support.

The figures in the foreground of the painting were first described in a rough sketch while I was talking to Major Keeble at Bruneval Barracks. Next I drew them out full-scale on tracing paper (which I hung in front of the full-size canvas) when we conferred again. We made certain changes, the need for which were now apparent on the larger scale. I had to learn exactly the varied duties and equipment of the Paras in action, so I was given a practical demonstration at Bruneval Barracks by a GPMG crew, a Milan team and a Blowpipe number. I conferred with the Harriers about their cluster-bomb attack, and with various additions, such as the casualty with a drip in the foreground, the whole was finally approved, and reproduced.

Living, as I do, in the New Forest the appearance of the burning gorse was something I already knew about.

The end of this stunning success was the surrender of some 1500 Argentinian defenders to the 500 exhausted but triumphant members of the Second Battalion, The Parachute Regiment.

23

24

23

Canberra and Queen Elizabeth II in Grytviken
– 28 May 1982

(Oil painting 16″ × 10″, property of P & O; second version at HMS Dryad)

No announcement was made of these ships meeting and exchanging passengers in South Georgia until *QE II* was only five days from her arrival back at Southampton, but on boarding her in the Channel I was able to learn from her Naval Liaison Staff (under Captain NCH James, RN) what she had been doing there. Awaiting her arrival in Grytviken had been *Canberra*, *Norland* and trawlers taken up from trade (one is alongside *QE II*). Waiting to embark the units of 5 Brigade she had ferried down from Southampton at high speed. In return she took aboard

from them for repatriation the survivors of HM Ships *Coventry*, *Antelope* and *Ardent*.

The steep-sided, mountainous appearance of South Georgia (rather like Norway) was long familiar to me from a lifetime of interest in the whole fishery based there, and its association with all Antarctic expeditions, especially that of Shackleton's dramatic arrival from Elephant Island in an open lifeboat. Once I had learned where the two big ships had lain at anchor, at what distance apart and what was their approximate heading, it was no problem to transpose them into the format of a small rough sketch. Two of the country's largest liners, scarcely entered upon their war service, meeting to exchange troops and survivors 8000 miles from home in such a setting, was maritime history.

24

'Goalkeeper' – South Atlantic – 1982

(Exploratory oil sketch 16″ × 10″, property of the Artist.
Oil painting 40″ × 26″, property of Vice-Admiral Sir John Woodward, KCB)

The safety of the two carriers *Hermes* and *Invincible* depended on a screen of destroyers and frigates dispersed across a wide area of the sea. The pattern of defence they presented to any attacker was designed to make best use of their varied armament, whether the attack came by air, surface ships or submarines.

The last line of surface defence depended on the

Goalkeeper, usually a Type 22 like *Brilliant* or *Broadsword*, whose close-range point defence Sea-Wolf was especially suited for the task of air defence. Inevitably it meant keeping very close indeed to the ships they were defending, and in thick weather this could cause some exciting moments. Fog in the South Atlantic could form and disperse very suddenly, swirling across the great seas of the South Atlantic which rolled up from the direction of Cape Horn. In such conditions the normal safety margins of ships keeping very close station were hard to maintain, but despite some close calls, no ship suffered any harm.

25

The Marine Commando Brigade's 'Jump' to Mount Kent
– 31 May 1982

(Exploratory oil sketch 16″ × 10″ property of the Artist, preparatory to finished painting)

There could be no advance by the British Army into Stanley until the crests of the mountains which overlooked the approaches had first been captured. Since early May, D Squadron of the SAS had been patrolling offensively in the area of the key Argentinian position on Mount Kent, far ahead of 3 Commando Brigade itself. They now concluded that the summit itself was held only lightly, if at all. It followed that if this far-advanced commanding point could be seized without delay, both the key to the Stanley defences and 3 Commando Brigade's advance would be secured at a single stroke.

The first attempt to airlift in troops of 42 Commando was frustrated by nil visibility. On 31 May two Sea-Kings of 846 Squadron lifted part of K Company 42 Commando, flying at only 20 feet over some 40 miles of

undulating ground, in the failing light of dusk. Promptly, on landing, and on meeting with their colleagues the SAS, a night attack was mounted which proved Mount Kent had now been abandoned. Within two hours the one surviving Chinook helicopter brought in three 105mm guns and 300 rounds of ammunition of 7 (Sphinx) Battery 29 Commando Regiment, Royal Artillery.

This move was supported by 3 Para who had thrust on on foot to reach Estancia House, in sight to the north-east of Mount Kent.

As dawn broke, those on the crest of the mountain could see down below them, only 12 miles away, the Moody Brook area close to Stanley where the Argentinians were believed to have a base camp. As one writer put it, 'It was an enormously exhilarating moment.' To give it added point, Sphinx Battery put down a few salvos on the distant enemy, to tell them they were now overlooked. Overnight they had been brought suddenly within range. The end, quite literally, was in sight.

25

26

Scots Guards' voyage to Bluff Cove
– 5 June 1982

(Oil painting 16″×10″, commissioned by Major Ewen Southby-Tailyour, OBE, RM. Original oil exploratory sketch 16″×10″, property of Fleet Air Arm Museum)

The advance by the Royal Marines and the Army across East Falkland to Stanley was made by 3 Commando Brigade (Royal Marines) in the north, and by 5 (Army) Brigade in the south. But it was difficult to co-ordinate the speed of the two, and when 2 Para leap-frogged a small force some thirty-five miles up to Fitzroy from Darwin on the south coast, it became vital to reinforce them quickly before the Argentinian Army counter-attacked in strength. Lacking airlift capacity, the only other way was by sea, so 600 Scots Guards were taken by the Assault Ship HMS *Intrepid* from San Carlos to a point near Lively Island whence, in darkness, they were to complete the final 35 miles of the voyage along the coast embarked in the four big Landing Craft (Utility), each carrying 150 men.

The Flotilla was launched successfully after dark on the night of 5/6 June, under the pilotage of the only man in the whole Task Force who, by happy chance, knew the unmarked, rocky, low-lying coast; knowledge gained during an earlier posting in command the Royal Marine Falkland detachment in 1978–9 and on which the whole planning of the landings depended. A dedicated explorer and cruising seaman (member of The Royal Cruising Club), Major Southby-Tailyour's time in the islands had been spent largely in surveying them from the viewpoint of his hobby. Never was time better spent on behalf of his country.

The overnight voyage was enlivened at one stage by being illuminated under star-shell fired by a Naval ship unaware of the plan and, later on, by the wind, which rose rapidly to strong gale force. The speed of the LCU's was reduced steadily until they were making only two to three knots over the ground. The wave-clutter made their radar ineffective at the short range needed for creeping along the shore, and their steering compasses could not be corrected beforehand to allow for the way they were loaded. But the key to success never escaped their grasp. The four craft managed to keep in visual contact with each other, and, as dawn was breaking over the tormented sea and even more tormented Guardsmen, the little Flotilla was guided safely through the narrow entrance of Bluff Cove, where the 600 men disembarked, without the loss of a single life.

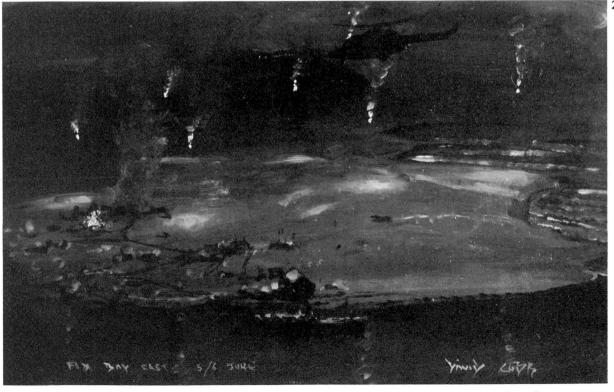

27

Bombardment of Fox Bay East
– 5/6 June 1982
(Exploratory oil sketch 16″ × 10″, property of Fleet Air Arm Museum)

The various Falkland settlements lie far apart, separated by many miles of featureless, undulating landscape and mountainside. The key to each land area is via the small groups of houses which are sited at a natural harbour. Such a one is Fox Bay, the main settlement in West Falkland. The Argentinian Army therefore made it their HQ, and protected it with extensive minefields, gun batteries, warning radars and defensive positions covering the southern sea approaches to Falkland Sound,

sited mainly in Fox Bay East.

This night bombardment by HMS *Avenger* of Fox Bay East was the fourth in a fortnight, in the course of which *Avenger*'s Lynx helicopter with the Naval Gunfire Forward Observer, Capt Harmes, RA, on board directing fire, was picked up by an Argentinian radar post ashore.

By pin-pointing the source of these radar transmissions Capt Harmes was able to instruct *Avenger* to fire upon it, after which the transmissions ceased. At the end of the campaign it was learnt that the radar had been hit by *Avenger* and so badly damaged that it was dropped useless into Fox Bay.

28

'Contrails'
(Oil exploratory sketch 16″ × 10″, property of Fleet Air Arm Museum)

Judged by the standards of the temperate zone of the Northern Hemisphere, the atmosphere of South Atlantic in the latitude of the Horn and the Falklands is remarkably clear. One consequence is that the condensation vapour trails or 'contrails' left by high-

flying aircraft are visible very much further in favourable conditions than they would be in Home Waters.

This fact was explained to me by Lt Cdr M Blissett, Senior Pilot of 800 Squadron (Sea Harriers), who referred to the consequent need for fighters approaching or leaving the Islands to fly an indirect course to and from the carriers, to avoid giving away their bearing to an observer on shore or airborne.

29 COLOUR

Sea Harrier Pursuit

(Exploratory oil sketch 16" × 10", property of Fleet Air Arm Museum)

The attacking aircraft left the Argentinian mainland at about 19,000 feet, but about fifty miles out from the Falklands they dropped to sea-level and below radar coverage, only re-appearing as they came in over the islands and from behind the hills. By then it was difficult to 'acquire' and then intercept them.

Almost all the interceptions by Sea Harriers of Argentinian fighter-bombers took place below 500 feet, with the enemy aircraft keeping low to avoid radar detection and being hit by missiles, and the Sea Harriers diving like hawks from their overhead Combat Air Patrols to intercept.

The Harrier weapon that accounted for most aircraft was the US Sidewinder AIM 9L air-to-air missile. This reported to the pilot by an audio tone in the pilot's head-phones when the hot exhaust of an enemy aircraft was being sensed, after which destruction was almost certain. The pilot listened for the sound which reported the missile 'locked on', after which he had only to fire and wait for the smoke trail of the missile to snake its way across the sky until it exploded on the target in a flash and a puff of smoke.

Despite this excellent weapon, the Argentinian attacks were often too numerous, and with the lack of airborne early warning radar, there was often insufficient time for the Harriers to be vectored to intercept before bombs were dropped. On the first day, twelve separate attacks were made, employing seventy-two aircraft. These were opposed by only three pairs of Harriers, capable of remaining on patrol only twenty minutes before they had to turn for home, when their places were taken by fresh pilots.

30

The First Harrier to Land in the Falklands – 5 June 1982

(Exploratory oil sketch 16" × 10", property of Fleet Air Arm Museum)

'When I'd climbed out, I found myself dancing a little jig...'

Harrier pilots on patrol over the Falklands had to conserve enough fuel to get them back to the carriers some 150–200 miles away to the east. This limited them to only about 20 minutes on patrol, before a fresh patrol had to take over, and they turned for home. Normally there were three such combat air patrols (CAPs) sited across the Falklands from north to south, totalling six aircraft, so involving eighteen in the course of each daylight hour. These had to be furnished from a total of only 30 in all, and even with 80% serviceability the strain of such a programme is clear.

When, for the first time, a Naval 'Harrier' was ordered to land at Port San Carlos airstrip, it signified –

i) that this invaluable aircraft and its highly-trained (and very successful) pilot were no longer at risk on the ground from air attack by the Argentinian Air Force;

ii) the San Carlos air defences were in command; and

iii) there was now an end to the strain of operating at such extreme pressure. (Hence the jig ... by Lt Cdr Thomas, CO 899 Squadron).

I was briefed on this background by the Senior Pilot of 800 Squadron Lt Cdr Blissett, who taught me the rudiments of the 'Sea Harrier' and its cockpit layout (after first ensuring that I had nothing in my pockets that could escape into the fuselage of the plane).

When, later, I visited the islands I asked the Pilot of HMS *Glasgow*'s Lynx to hover over the airstrip at Port San Carlos while I drew it against the background of San Carlos Water and, beyond it, Falkland South and West Falkland, whence we had just flown.

This was an opportunity to show the general features of the area as well as a significant moment in the campaign.

TUCY SAN CARLOS - 1ST HARRIER LANDING

SIR GALAHAD RESCUE

31

The Attack on RFA's Sir Galahad
– 8 June 1982
and *Sir Tristram* at Fitzroy
(Exploratory oil sketch 16″ × 10″, property of Fleet Air Arm Museum)
The two Landing Ships Logistic (LSL) *Sir Galahad* and *Sir Tristram* were attacked from the air and hit by bombs when lying at anchor in Port Pleasant, close to Fitzroy Settlement (often referred to inaccurately as Bluff Cove in this context); 51 men died and a number were injured in this attack, carried out by two Skyhawks and two Mirages aircraft. As in most setbacks, a number of

different causes together led to this sad episode. If the day had been misty, with low visibility, probably it would never have happened because the two ships would not have been located in the first place. In that case the decision to send them so far ahead of the rest of 5 Brigade would have been hailed as a master-stroke.

The brunt of the loss was suffered by the Welsh Guards aboard *Sir Galahad*, who were waiting to get ashore. Helicopters were quickly on the scene to recover men from on board and from the water. These air crews showed a fine disregard for danger in hovering close to the burning ship, aboard which ammunition was exploding, in order to carry out their work of rescue.

32

3 Commando Brigade across the Falklands
(Exploratory oil sketch 16″ × 10″, property of Vice-Admiral Sir John Woodward, KCB. Copy: property of P Pollock, Esq)
When the large transport ship *Atlantic Conveyor* was sunk to the north of the Falklands by Exocet on 25 May, three of the four big Chinook helicopters she had been carrying sank with her. At 80-men-a-time, the lifting power of these huge machines had been key factors in planning the Brigade's advance on Stanley across East Falkland, and – keeping it properly supplied. It was vital that the troops

be maintained in fighting form, and were not exhausted by first crossing on foot some 50 miles of the barren, bleak uplands of the harsh landscape. Now they had to do so.

I had flown low over the line of their advance from Port San Carlos Settlement on my return trip to Stanley, passing over Teal Inlet, and seeing to the south of me those now-famous mountains. As a forced march, carrying 120lb each, it was a formidable feat to cross the sleet, rain and snowswept moorland, and in conversation with Major-General Thompson who, as a Brigadier, commanded the Brigade, I came to the conclusion that

these solitary files in open order laden like mules and stretching out of sight into the mists ahead, epitomised the soldier's war just as much as did the very skilled and courageous hand-to-hand night-fighting with which they ended it.

The rivalry which exists between different units in the Services is common to all the armed forces of history.

That which enlivens the Marines and the Parachutists, and such units as the SAS and SBS, spurs each on to out-do the others; but in this case its effect was to reinforce the collective will to lose no time in rolling up an enemy who had put them to such extremes of hardship. There was only one way of ending the discomfort, and that was forward.

33

Attack by The Third Battalion, The Parachute Regiment on Mount Longdon
– 11 June 1982

(Oil painting 16″×10″, commissioned by the officers of the Battalion. Property of Lt Col Hew Pike, DSO, MBE)

Soon after the end of the Falklands campaign the Commander Officer of the Third Battalion, Lt Col Hew Pike left the Battalion and his officers presented him with a painting to commemorate the events of the previous summer. Responsibility for organising this was in the hands of Lt Andrew Mills, 3 Para, who kindly helped me with the painting, and paid me several visits while it was in preparation.

Mount Longdon was one of several mountains lying to the west of Stanley, each of which had been turned into a strongly-fortified and well-sited pattern of defence which commanded all the approaches to the harbour and the town. The early reduction of these strongpoints without delay was essential. The Landing Force supply lines were at full stretch, ammunition was only just sufficient and the harsh physical strain imposed by the exposed uplands was certain to take its toil of the troops if the battle went on for long.

The chosen method depended for success on first-class training and morale. It consisted of a continuous series of night attacks, and the painting shows 3 Para moving into the attack after a four-hour night approach march under the brooding threat of Mount Longdon where their battle was to be fought and won. In the course of it Sergeant McKay won a posthumous VC, one of two awarded during the campaign.

33

34

The Battle for Two Sisters seen beyond LSL Sir Galahad at Fitzroy
– 11 June 1982
(Exploratory oil sketch 16″×10″, property of Fleet Air Arm Museum)

This sketch was in response to the description given to me by Sub Lt Humphreys and Lt Middleton of 846 Squadron (Sea Kings) in reply to my question about what stuck most clearly in their minds in all that they had soon.

As they flew towards the distant mountains surrounding Stanley, some now held by the British, their course led them over Fitzroy Settlement and Port Pleasant where the LSL's *Sir Galahad* and *Sir Tristram* had been attacked three days previously, from the former of which smoke was still rising.

Suddenly there broke out on the horizon ahead of them an intense exchange of fire at the crest of Two Sisters Mountain. Here 45 Commando were setting about dislodging the Argentinian defenders from their entrenchments, aided by the supporting gunfire of HMS *Glamorgan* from seawards.

34

35
1st Battalion, The Welsh Guards
move off towards Stanley
– 11 June 1982

(Oil painting 40"×20" commissioned by the Regiment. Exploratory oil sketch 18"×7", property of the Artist)

From the initial landings in San Carlos Water there was a choice of two approaches to Stanley, 50 miles away to the East. The more direct one, along which 3 Brigade had already advanced, keeps to the North of the mountainous Wickham Heights. The longer, half as far again and allotted to 5 Brigade, sweeps southwards in a semi-circle via Darwin and Fitzroy.

In order to reinforce the impending attack on the Stanley defences, it was essential to combine and so maximise the impact of two Brigades. 5 Brigade's later arrival from South Georgia could only be offset by embarking them afresh overnight to bring them in line with 3 Commando Brigade. This entailed a sea move around to Fitzroy and Bluff Cove.

From prior discussion with the CO of the Welsh Guards, Lt Col Johnny Rickett, and from a study of the terrain just inland of Bluff Cove, I painted this study of the track to Stanley and the Battalion moving off in the late afternoon of 11 June. Above on the left are the slopes of Mt Challenger. Under command of 3 Commando Brigade they were about to attack the Harriet/Two Sisters/Mt Longdon line, and were being subjected to harassing fire from the 155mm Argentine artillery 12–15 miles away.

In the foreground is an example of the unique geological feature of the Falklands. These 'stone runs' are areas of random blocks of granite which lie across the landscape like broad streams of petrified, splintered lava. They are covered in lichen, are extremely slippery when wet, and are hazardous to cross even in daytime. In darkness they are formidable obstacles to any infantry, weighted down with equipment, advancing in open order, across whose path they lay.

35

36

MV Elk and HM Ships Exeter and Fearless
– 12 June 1982

(Oil painting 30″×24″, property of P & O Steamship Company)
The P & O Company commissioned four paintings each 30″×24″ and purchased two pilot-studies to show the very distinguished and essential service rendered by 'ships taken up from trade' (STUFT) of which *Elk* was the first. She was also the first to join the RN Task Force, became known as 'The Toybox' and, due to her helicopter maintenance capabilities and very active service, she was nick-named later HMS *Elk Royal*. She was also classified as a 'high value unit' on account of her cargo, the ammunition component of which started at 350 tons but totalled 2200 tons by the time she sailed from Southampton.

On her way south, at Ascension Island, all but a short section of her bulwarks were sliced off and dropped overboard, to allow her to land the large Chinook helicopters on deck. Two Bofors guns were also fitted forward, to give her some self-defence.

Elk's first run into San Carlos Water was on the night 27–28 May, the second on the night of 30 May; but she stayed all day 31 May. In all she made five runs until on 12 June she was lying in her usual berth off Fern Valley Creek when the last Argentinian air attack was detected approaching at high level, where HMS *Exeter*'s Sea Dart found a solution at long range and brought down the plane.

In planning the painting I was concerned to show as much as possible of the work of the ship, (helicopters on deck, etc., bulwarks shorn off, stern gate open and Mexeflote approaching) and something of the anchorage position she occupied; but to prevent the scene being too static (always a pictorial problem with ships at anchor in smooth water as in three out of four P & O paintings) I took a slight liberty by strengthening the breeze from the North, and suggesting a rainsquall behind *Exeter*.

Elk's Master, Captain John Morton, kindly helped me in assembling the facts both of his own service and on that of other ships, but particularly about the whole area of operations, where he had served previously in the British Antarctic Survey.

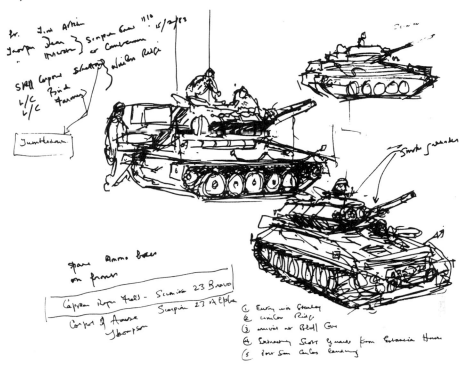

37

Attack by the Second Battalion, The Parachute Regiment on Wireless Ridge

– 13 June 1982

(Oil painting 50″ × 40″, commissioned by The Second Battalion, The Parachute Regiment)

Wireless Ridge stands about three miles north-west of Stanley, and was one of the semi-circle of fortified mountain ridges which made up the defensive perimeter of the town. Each terminated at its crest in abrupt craggy stone outcrops, among which dug-outs and sangars were hidden.

The chosen method of attack was by a 'four-phase, noisy, night attack'. It was supported by 2 batteries of 105mm guns 29 (Corunna) Battery and 97 (Lawson's) Battery of the Field Regiment, RA, HMS *Ambuscade*'s 4.5, the mortars of 2 and 3 Para, also the Machine Gun Platoon. Very different from Goose Green, in fact.

The scene is just after 0400 and the fourth phase of the attack is in progress. A and B Companies have secured their phase two objective and are seen in the painting sheltering among the snow-sprinkled peat hags from the Argentinian artillery fire. They had been joined by the

Scorpion and Scimitar light tanks of The Blues and Royals (visible on the left of the painting) and the six GPMG (SFs) of the Machine Gun Platoon which are just beyond the brow of the slope in the foreground.

A Milan anti-tank missile is being fired, and covering fire is being given to D Company who are assaulting from the right of the scene, along the final ridge line before Port Stanley.

Overhead the star-shell from the Navy lights up the defences of Wireless Ridge across the mist-filled valley. On the left are just visible the lights of Stanley, and on the right can be seen the first signs of the flank attack by D Company.

The painting was developed first from sketches made in my sketch-book while on a visit to 2 Para at Bruneval Barracks. Next I drew out full-scale on tracing paper, the gist of what I had learned, and finally the CO, Lt Colonel Chaundler, and I re-adjusted the features until they seemed about right.

Finally I took the semi-finished painting up to Aldershot, where all the other officers who took part in the attack were able to study the effect and pass comment.

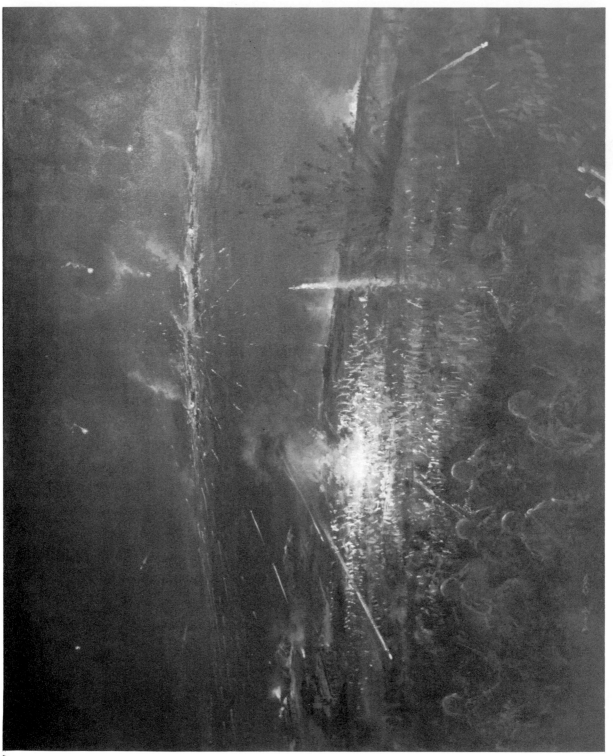

38

Lycaon at San Carlos

– 14 June 1982

(Oil painting 26"×18", commissioned by Ocean Transport and Trading plc)

Lycaon, an Elder Dempster Lines ship, was lying in reserve at Falmouth when, on 27 April she was chartered by the MOD for service in the Falklands. She sailed to Southampton for fitting of RAS gear and loading with 2000 tons of ammunition and 3000 tons of general supplies. She also loaded a small RCT harbour tug and two LCVs on deck. She sailed from Southampton on 4 May, picked up more supplies, tents and missiles etc at Ascension, and proceeded to South Georgia, which she approached through low visibility, icebergs and growlers, arriving at Stromness Harbour on 28 May.

Here she transferred stores and ammunition to the RFA *Blue Rover* until that ship was full and sailed for the Falklands. *Lycaon* continued unloading into the trawlers *Farnella* and *Junella* until she was warned of submarine threat and ordered to hide in the ice-pack 60 miles or so to the north-east. She returned on 31 May. Next came strong winds, gusting without warning to Forces 9 and 10.

Then more unloading until 8 June, when *Lycaon* sailed for the Falklands, first to rendezvous with HMS *Glamorgan* to transfer mail on 11 June, some 200 miles east of the islands.

The last air-raid of the war took place on the early morning of 14 June as *Lycaon* approached San Carlos and HMS *Cardiff* shot down a plane some 40 miles to the west, but at 1040 *Lycaon* finally anchored close to HMS *Engadine* (in the painting, just beyond and to the right of her). Further away to the north and north-west (from right to left) are HMS *Cardiff*, *Baltic Ferry*, RFA *Olna* and RFA *Sir Perceval*.

Early in 1983 I was asked by Ocean Transport & Trading, plc to accept this commission to commemorate *Lycaon*'s Falkland service. With the kind help of her Master, Captain HR Lawton, whom I visited in Yorkshire, I was able to assemble the data which led to the picture above.

Port Stanley and Port William – 20 June 1982
(Exploratory sketch 16"×10", property of the Artist)

The Argentinian surrender on 14 June made it possible
to bring round to Port Stanley much of the supply fleet
which had been lying in San Carlos. There was insufficient space and water for the larger ships to enter Port
Stanley itself, but outside lay the larger roadstead called
Port William. This was sheltered from all quarters
except the east, so here, and in Port Stanley, anchored
23 varied merchant ships, which was by far the largest
fleet that had ever been seen in the Falklands. There
was no Port War Signal Station to allot an anchor berth
to each ship, or to record its exact time of arrival and
departure, but before going to the Falklands I had been
asked by the P & O Company to paint the four of their
ships together, so this great gathering seemed likely to
be the one occasion when, in fact, they were in
company.

With this in mind I took the first chance to draw the
shape of the port as it appeared from the hovering
Gazelle which was later to fly me to Fitzroy. It
transpired later that the four ships never were close
enough together to make one picture; but it also turned
out that an ex-Marine and long-time resident of Port
Stanley, Mr John Smith, was fully alive to the historic
importance of this event, and had made careful notes of
it at the time. He was generous enough to communicate
the results to me, and from this I developed the preliminary sketch. The ships concerned were these:

PORT WILLIAM (foreground)	PORT STANLEY (background)
Iris	Tor Caledonia
Astronomer	Baltic Ferry
G A Walker	Typhoon
RFA Fort Toronto	St Edmund
Geesport	Norland
Lycaon	HMS Junella
Laertes	HMS Fenella
Atlantic Causeway	HMS Pict
Canberra	Elk
Uganda	LSL Sir Perceval
Contender Bezant	LSL Sir Geraint
HMS Avenger (Guardship)	Europic Ferry

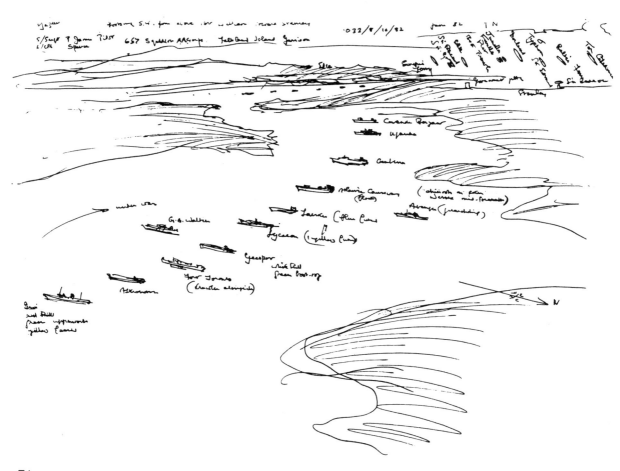

Canberra's Return to Southampton – 11 July 1982
*(Exploratory oil sketch 16″ × 10″, purchased by P & O
Steamship Co. Ltd
Copies: Fleet Air Arm Museum; Mrs D Mowlam)*

Canberra, known familiarly as 'The Great White
Whale' returned safely to Southampton, with three
months and 25,245 miles of War Service behind her
since she had sailed. She had survived unscathed an
astonishing day of air attacks in San Carlos. A simple
sum showed that, had she been sunk there, her
upperworks (had she sunk upright) would have
remained above water; but (remembering the 3000 men
lost from liner *Lancastria* alone, off St Nazaire in 1940)
her return with the 2500 men of 3 Brigade safely
aboard, their distant campaign bravely won, ensured a
welcome few ships can never have received.

The morning was beautifully warm, and as the ship
approached via the east end of the Isle of Wight, a small
armada began to gather round her, to escort her the last
few miles home. They were soon joined by light
aircraft. Finally, the Prince of Wales accompanied by

the Commander-in-Chief Fleet, and the Commandant
General of the Royal Marines, joined her by helicopter.

All along the shorelines huge crowds had gathered.
The police soon gave up estimating at over 35,000
people waiting on the Southampton quays. The light
mist in Southampton Water kept visibility down to
about 1½ miles, so that the liner and her flotilla of
escorting small craft loomed into sight very
impressively at surprisingly short range. Suddenly there
she was. Astern followed the P & O ferry *Dragon*. All
around the crews of tugs (hoses playing), yachts
(hooters blowing) and craft of every imaginable type,
cheered, shouted and waved.

I had taken a position on top of an abandoned
quayside shed, near the dockhead. This gave an
uninterrupted view over the heads of onlookers. I used
a small 16″ × 10″ panel to paint in an impression of the
crowd, as the ship (obligingly slowly) came into view
against the morning sun. It was a vivid scene of life and
movement in which the reserved British really gave
vent to their feelings.

41

137 BATTERY R.A.
FITZROY SETTLEMENT
1430/8/12/82

DAVID COBB

42

1615/11/10/82

(STKES) A.D. BATTERY (28 BRAVO)
RADAR FIRE UNIT WITH D.N. IAI
SAN CARLOS. FALKLAND ISLANDS.

DAVID COBB

41

Fitzroy under snow 'No Flying'
–1430/8 October 1982
(*Oil preliminary sketch 16″×10″, property of Fleet Air Arm Museum. Copy: property 136 (Java) Battery*)
'...when they see your sketch maybe they'll realise what life can be like down here...'
  Major J Tulloch RA (CO 136 (Java) Battery)
  Returning on foot through the snow from the Welsh Guards Memorial and the neighbouring stores dump, I took a short cut back towards the causeway-bridge

below the Shearing Shed. At the top of the hill I saw across the creek the Settlement at Fitzroy, with the guns of the Battery just visible on the crest of the hill, and a grounded Wessex awaiting a clearance in the weather to continue its flight.
  The lowering look of the snow-filled sky was a reminder of the campaigning conditions, whether experienced by sea or land. This was exactly what I had come to see for myself, and with the snowflakes falling on my drawing and on the preliminary sketch, I worked at speed to catch the moment.

42

Rapier Site 23 Bravo, San Carlos Water
– 11 October 1982
(*Exploratory oil sketch 16″×10″, property of Fleet Air Arm Museum. Copy: property 58 (Eyre's) Air Defence Battery, 12 Air Defence Regiment, RA*)
The mountains which surround San Carlos Water are some 1000–1500 feet high, run almost continuously the full length of each side and across its ends. They formed a good natural obstacle against bombing attack by low-flying aircraft, but very soon the Argentinian Air Force learned that the Fleet's air defence of all types deserved respect if they took the risk of flying high. As a result they returned to very low level attacks, and so lost accuracy and also the time-lapse needed to arm the bombs.
  In the heat of action few things are more difficult to

analyse than the conflicting claims to have brought down planes, and after the campaign ended, five hitherto uncounted aircraft were located in the vicinity of Falkland Sound alone.
  The Rapier Batteries, of which 23 Bravo was one, the Navy's guns and missile systems, the Landing Forces' small arms and hand-guided missiles were at times all operating simultaneously, with results that will probably never be known for certain, because nobody can be certain which scored the vital hit; or whether it was a culmination of damage which proved effective. Moreover it is very natural for two different defence systems which both register hits on an attacking aircraft which is shot down, for both claim it as their own unaided success.

43 COLOUR

Her Majesty's Ship Junella at Sea
(*Exploratory oil sketch 16″×10″, property of Vice-Admiral Sir John Woodward, KCB*)
The smallest merchant ships to join the Task Force were five deep-sea commercial trawlers of 1200–1500 tons and speeds up to 17 knots: fine, tough seaboats which carried fuel for two months at sea. All were taken up from fishing between 13–20 April to be fitted specially as minesweepers for deep-water mines (EDATS), being manned by Royal Navy crews to form the 11th Minesweeping Squadron wearing the White Ensign. (Their normal crews argued strenuously to be

allowed to go to the Falklands, and to take their nets too!).
  For three months with little support they carried out tasks which ranged from cross-decking personnel between *Canberra* and *QE II* in Grytviken, South Georgia, to special operations as yet unspecified around the Falklands, and in the main San Carlos landings. Finally, they swept successfully for the mines laid by the Argentinians.
  I made this preliminary sketch of *Junella*, owned by J Marr and Sons of Hull, to give an idea of how big seas can treat small ships, and as a reminder of the traditional Naval use of Fishing Vessels in time of war.

44 COLOUR

HMS Cardiff's 'Feu de Joie' – 14 June 1982
(*Exploratory sketch 16″×10″, property of Vice-Admiral Sir John Woodward, KCB*)
When the weary Land Forces had entered Port Stanley after their gruelling capture of the Argentinian mountain defences, far out at sea aboard the ships the

news of the Argentinian surrender was greeted with profound relief. *Cardiff*, steaming on *Hermes*' starboard bow made her contribution in traditional style by mustering every possible firearm around the upper deck, and despatching a celebratory cone of tracer into the evening sky. This sketch was the artist's first attempt to interpret the description given him by the

Task Force Commander, Vice-Admiral Sir John Woodward only shortly before this book went to press, to see whether this very significant moment could be caught.

For the Admiral, who had never been able to see the victory he had brought about, it was a moment of surreal beauty, superimposing the relief of victory upon the menace of warfare.

10.30 MPA opening by aim of Prince

45 COLOUR

Opening of Mount Pleasant Airport by HRH Prince Andrew

– 12 May 1985

(Oil painting 30″×12″, commissioned by Mowlem International Limited)

The airport was constructed by a consortium of John Laing, John Mowlem and Amey Roadstone Construction, usually known as LMA. It is located on a greenfield site some 50 kilometres from Port Stanley and was constructed at an exceptionally fast rate. The logistical problems of supplying all materials other than stone and water from Britain, a distance of 7000 nautical miles, were formidable and the weather conditions are far from ideal. As an 'Instant' port LMA established a floating bridgehead in East Cove in October 1983 by attaching the MV *Merchant Providence* to the shore with two struts and a Bailey Bridge. Work commenced on the runway some 8 kilometres away in January 1984. The main runway is 2590 metres in length and the secondary 1525 metres. The airport's major buildings comprise a hangar capable of housing a Tristar, power station and standby, control tower, living accommodation for over 2000 people and fuel installations situated at Mare Harbour connected by pipeline to the field. In addition there is some 40 kilometres of access and perimeter roads on the site and a new highway over peat bogs to Port Stanley.

The picture depicts the Tristar hangar in left foreground and Search & Rescue Hangar left centre. On the main apron, which will finally stretch further to the left, stands the first Tristar to land formally; the line of the main runway is seen in centre and a road of 8 kilometres leading northwards to the quartzite quarry on the western shoulder of Mount Pleasant. This quarry provides all the hard rock required for runway pavements and structural concrete. In the background Mount Wickham is often snow-covered.

This was the scene in early May 1985 at Mount Pleasant on the landing of the first wide-bodied jet and at the time of the formal opening by HRH Prince Andrew, some 16 months after commencement of work on the runway. A remarkable achievement.

46

Mare Harbour Wharf under construction by George Wimpey/ Taylor Woodrow joint venture

– 12 May 1985

(Exploratory oil sketch 20″×12″, property of the Artist)

To supply fuel and freight requirements to Mount Pleasant Airport, a joint venture of George Wimpey and Taylor Woodrow contracted to build a permanent deep-water (9m) wharf at Mare Harbour, close to the temporary berth in East Cove occupied by *Merchant Providence*.

The method used sheet-piling driven in a circle to form caissons. Alongside the first caisson, second, third and fourth caissons were formed until a line of seven such caissons each interlocked with its neighbour gave a solid wharf some 500 feet in length. At the start of each new caisson a circular steel template was positioned to help retain the circular shape.

On completion, the wharf provides not only a quayside, but also additional mooring dolphins, sited ahead and astern to allow ships longer than 500 feet to lie securely alongside.

In the first stage of construction, infilling the caisson with granular material was by crane and grab, working off a floating pontoon; but as soon as two caissons were in position, the approach route from the shore was completed and allowed the caissons to be filled by either crane or conveyor.

When it is finished, the permanent wharf at Mare Harbour is to include fuel storage tanks and warehousing sited on the nearby shore.

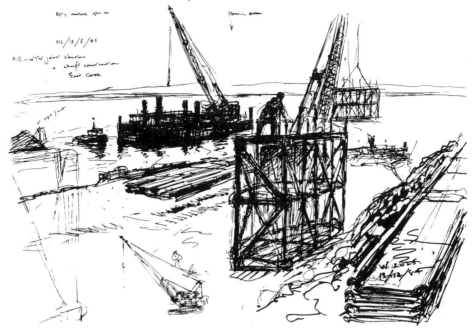

46

MV Merchant Providence moored in East Cove, Falkland Islands

– 1983

(Oil painting 30″×16″, commissioned by John Laing Construction Ltd. Exploratory oil-sketch 30″ × 12″ property of the Artist)

This 13,000 ton vessel was built in Hamburg in 1965, and on purchase by the Laing-Mowlem-ARC Joint Venture in mid-1983 work was immediately put in hand to adapt her as a beach-head and unloading facility. Structural alterations were made to 3 and 4 holds to create a large, flush deck-space specially strengthened for manoevring vehicles.

The chosen berth in East Cove had a depth of 9 metres close enough to the shore for vehicles to be driven across via a Bailey Bridge; and the ship was held permanently in this offshore position by two 50m tubular struts in addition to heavy moorings laid out ahead and astern.

For the initial stages of the work she was adapted to accommodate 100 men and her galley was extended to cope with 300 and 2000 tonnes of fuel were stored. On arrival at East Cove in late October 1983, less than four months later, she was carrying on deck and below all the necessary plant and materials needed for the installation of the ship as a jetty-head, and for the construction of the 7km access road up to the site chosen for the airport.

To administer and monitor this operation as it progressed *Merchant Providence* was fitted with a Marasat telephone-telex system using satellites linked to all international communications.

This concept of a ship-converted-to-a-jetty is far from new, but in the Falklands (where it had been used for very many years) it was especially valuable on this remote, uninhabited, roadless, windswept, coast. For LMA it enabled heavy plant to drive straight ashore from the ship to start work; meanwhile she provided the construction crews with a warm, solid base from which to operate.

Ships berthing alongside *Merchant Providence* ranged from the 8000 tonne MV *England* which ferried construction personnel between Capetown and the Falklands, to larger freighters bringing up to 30,000 freight tonnes in supplies and stores direct from the United Kingdom.

48

Amey Roadstone Corporation Quartzite Quarry Mount Pleasant

(Exploratory oil study 16″×10″, property of the Artist)

The success of the enterprise depended on a massive supply of suitable quarried material. Almost all of the stone, (some 1.5 million tonnes in April 1985) including aggregates for pavement-quality concrete; structural concrete and asphalt paving was quarried and processed by LMA on the Island. The quartzite quarry, shown here, near the top of Mount Pleasant ridge, overlooks the distant airport and the coast at East Cove some 10 miles away.

The series of levels which characterise the face of a quarry are known as 'benches'; and, as the painting shows, on the bench being worked in the foreground the drills are preparing the way for the charges needed to blast away the next step into the rock-face. When the material broken away by the blast has been gathered, it is transported to the processing plant for conversion into the appropriate grade.

To forecast accurately the potential yield of a quarry and identify its quality is an important professional skill. MPA needed roughly 1.2 million tonnes of tillite and .5 million tonnes of quartzite, but in the later search for aggregates a number of additional 'borrow' pits were established as well as fresh quarries along the 30 mile road to Stanley.

Falklands Diary

5/10/82

1000   Soon after leaving Brize Norton (the VC-10 of RAF more or less the same as the civil version) we climbed up steeply from cloud into sun. The Welsh (?) coast was visible in patches, but I couldn't be sure where.

By 1030 we were turning south, and soon after I paid an (invited) visit up forward, to talk for 10–15 minutes with the pilot. I think I was the only one to do so. The passengers are all three Services, plus one merchant seaman in search of his container ship somewhere off Falklands.

The cloud cover was fairly continuous beneath us at our height of 35,000 feet and 550 mph. Except for some dark strips of cirrus on the horizon, the whole looking brilliant under an almost clear sky.

I had won a window seat, just ahead of the starboard wing; but all seats face aft, for safety reasons, and I don't care for it – I like to see what's ahead, in all possible subjects!

Packaged food plus snacks arrived steadily throughout the flight, but Oh, for a deep draught of anything fresh! Perhaps they want to keep down the rate of 'heads' use . . .

My neighbour was a PO Technician rejoining his ship after 14 days compassionate leave at Pompey, trying to save his marriage from going bust. A nice, broad-faced, good-featured, strongly-built chap, going for Chief soon.

The cloud beneath us allowed glimpses of the sea, with a strong NW wind and white caps. At our height the wind speed is over 200 knots, just aft of the beam, needing a 15–20 degree correction (?) to the course. Later, as we ran down towards the African coast, I realised that it is just 41½ years since I was last here,

steaming south at nine knots aboard *Canna*, escorting the valuable heavy-lift ship *Belnor*, and three small whalers, down to Freetown. The little Trade-wind clouds, low on the surface (you could see their shadows, now that the sun was getting overhead) were still chasing one another down the coast – nothing much had changed that I could see (except me, and this astonishing jet-plane full of people!).

We turned in to the coast, dropped down through cloud as we lost height, to land at Dakar at 1430 to refuel. I could not see the expected Naval harbour we attacked in 1940; only a commercial port sited on the side of what appeared to be a wide river – all that happened was suddenly, instead of sea, we had a low, flat coast close beneath us, with an onshore breeze sending in breakers onto a sandy beach.

We landed, and taxied round to an isolated patch of tarmac. While the bowsers did their work we were all allowed to stand around near the plane and stretch our cramped legs. Most stood. I found I *had* to walk.

Rain had fallen recently – the atmosphere was close and damp, overcast, and only too familiar – West Africa!

Sandy soil was growing lots of things I couldn't recognise, but I found two noble designs of grasshopper. A green one, like our own, but about 2in to 2½in long, which fairly leapt when of a mind to do so, covering about 6–7 feet. A smaller, brown one was too well-camouflaged to see its design properly, but it seemed to have wings of a kind which allowed it to soar, and alter course in mid-air.

The airfield had spread over a large area in the way airfields do, the odd building here and there seeming irrelevant and superseded; only the control tower and its vicinity showing signs of civic pride. There was a good covering of greenery, but trees were poorish specimens. On top of a tall, volcanic 'tump' of 200 feet stood the lighthouse, the only elevated bit of ground, just outside the airfield perimeter. A row of three sagging, cannibalised Dakotas gave the place an air of neglect, and I wondered whether the black gentlemen who drove the bowser were happier for the white man's arrival. Not knowing what their earlier life was like it's hard to say, but *Canna*'s three Krooboy Stokers were merry all the time, and I hoped these were too.

Whoosh off into the sky again – this time the sun getting into the west and its light falling on top of the little clouds 'contre jour', like the tops of so many mushrooms.

We reached Wideawake Airport at Ascension about 1830 (or is it 1930 ? – these time changes are difficult to follow) in darkness, which fell upon us suddenly as we lost height. Splendid tropical colours turning to dark purple, and, as we landed, we found the runway driven between steep volcanic craters rising steeply close on either side to some 1500ft, very sudden and dramatic.

It was eerie – just like Gibraltar in 1941 ... Servicemen in shorts and desert boots – brown, loquacious, fraternal – drifting in groups to and fro under the glare of arc-lights; relaxed, self-confident, totally competent.

We were driven off across the island in 3-ton lorries to a very primitive transit camp – my first ever, and certainly broadening to the mind; but I found a wash-house, had a shave and a wash, and with two tins of beer inside, slept on a battered camp bed for three hours or so, until muster at 0230. My soldier colleagues all sprang like gazelles up the sides of the lorries, tossing their gear ahead. I tried to do the same, meanwhile preserving my precious sketching gear which wasn't easy.

Back in the dark to the airfield; breakfast in a field kitchen and a walk back to the briefing hangar. The island is wholly volcanic, dust everywhere you walk, but a ton of money has made it into a sophisticated communications base, with barracks, air-field, workshops, etc. No indigenous inhabitants and I think nothing useful grows. The one or two trees that I saw had sturdy trunks, tapering rapidly into a broad bushy top, only 7–8 feet high, presumably to conserve moisture.

0530/6   Our take-off in the Hercules ... a real war-horse of a transport plane, with huge, cavernous, square-section insides, *loaded* with stuff, seats down each side, not *too* bad, but I took advice and forsook mine to build a private billet among some kit-bags where I slept happily for about two hours, until the Loadmaster found me, and (very politely) asked me to rest elsewhere, as the kit might contain crushable items. So I

got up, and began to write this account – feeling much spryer than I expected. It's a lovely sunny morning 20,000 feet above the South Atlantic, and my worries (about proving a burden to my hosts in any way) have, at least temporarily, vanished. The trouble is that they are all 30–40 years younger than me, and in peak of condition. Never mind, the one woman aboard is a nice-looking sort of RAF Matron/Sister (the focus of much curiosity) – if I feel frail maybe she'll hold my hand until I feel better!

1040   We refuelled (from another Hercules I believe) at about 0930, but I failed to 'book-in' to watch it from the cockpit, not realising that there would be a queue, so I've also missed the later 'Victor' refuelling too, though this aspect of my trip is not a vital one, and I gather one can see a lot from the portholes. The need for refuelling on the outward leg to the Falklands, and not the homeward, is to retain enough fuel aboard the Hercules to allow for a diversion if necessary, when Argentina and much of Latin-America is 'out of bounds', or better avoided. This I learned from a later visit to the cockpit, providing a wonderful view across what looked like an ice-field, except that the occasional 'bergs' have round tops.

The second pilot (co-pilot ?) was easy to hear, and gave the above information plus much else. The crew does alternate months flying Hercules from AI to F about every two days. It's a very costly process, as there are only about 50 passengers and a few tons of stores but apparently *Norland* which is doing the sea run, and takes about a fortnight, is too large, and takes too long to fill up.

At 1230 we RVZ with our Vulcan to refuel us. She took up a steady course and speed, and the Hercules closed up slowly from astern about 25 feet (?) below, until about a length astern, but both diving slowly (called 'tobogganning') to allow the 380 mph Hercules to match the Vulcan's minimum of 400 mph. There was some rhythmic turbulence from the slipstream, but not excessive. Fifteen minutes later, among some superb clouds, the Vulcan slipped the tow and wheeled away to port, which gave me a good view of her. I had been able to see part of her wings and spare fuel-pods, etc. when refuelling was in progress.

1330   Talking to a helo-repair team of three from Lee-on-Solent, coming out to rebuild the fractured tail-hinge of a Wessex. The Engineer Officer in charge (unsure of his rank) is by way of being a cartoonist, and left the Service some years ago to turn professional, but I think it didn't work. (Hard to hear what people are saying). Afterwards I looked out to a new form of cloudscape, *so* like a wet pavement or mud, but, in fact, one was seeing through to the lower layer of cumulus below the stratus.

The Loadmaster has just (1430) handed out a *second* box of lunch, which consists of boiled egg, two large sandwiches, fruit juice, chunks of fried chicken, etc, etc. I'd just finished my fried egg and bacon sandwiches from home, so I've stowed away this new manna against the morrow. LM tells me to visit the cockpit if I wish, any time, but this means some 25 people have to stop snoozing and move their legs to let me pass, and then wake up again ten minutes later to let me back, so I desist. The homeward flights usually offer a little more room, maybe I'll try again then. I asked the LM what loads he has carried. They can load a Wessex, minus rotor head, Lynx, etc, 3-ton lorries, and 60 (?) parachutists can drop out in 30 seconds via both sides and back. Last week he loaded chicks, plus vet to look after them!

Outside the cloud top is at our level, so you can't see much except white. We are meeting those Trade Winds blowing up from the Horn which made progress so difficult and slow for the square-riggers bound west, and they are strong enough to slow us down too.

We came down with a thump at Stanley, bright and cold, about 1730, and at my residence Sparrowhawk House I met Major Gordon Crumley, Permanent President Courtmartial, based at York.

John Smith, ex-Marine, ex-British Antarctic Survey, ex-Falkland Island Company, married to an Islander, proved to be my excellent and most interesting host; now running this small guest-house at Stanley where Crumley is staying, a lively fellow-guest on a tour of duty.

I was driven here by Lt Cdr Nigel Maddox (who is fixing my affairs) past endless debris of war and peace; but behind it, to the west, was a spectacular sweep of low moors and scree, rising sharply to sharp outcrops of granite at the summit of distant mountain tops. Sunny, but cold, with a light NW breeze.

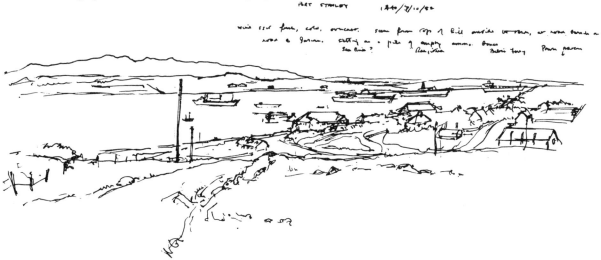

7/10/82

As the Argentinians have left it, roads all broken up, etc, Stanley is a dump. But it's on a wonderful island. The trouble, I imagine, is that there is insufficient attraction to bring people in to a small distant world sans TV, supermarkets, no milk, no papers, etc. I would need to have a compelling aim of some kind to live here. John Smith's is that of marine antiquarian, his little house *filled* with marine articles of every conceivable type, mostly 19th century, mostly collected from around the islands. He is also a model-maker, map-maker and artist; designer of Falkland Island stamps.

After a quick run round (very depressing, really) and posting a letter, I returned to find Colin Nicol and Bob Headland, both of British Antarctic Survey, Grytviken, South Georgia, installed for two nights.

Soon after lunch I set off afresh, the weather tending to clear. The house faces north, towards the sun, so there is no bother in getting orientated, as I had expected.

First I visited LSL *Sir Tristram*; bomb-damaged, alongside, serving as an accommodation ship; then back, to the west, out of the town up the road towards Sapper Hill and Darwin (minefield each side) for a drawing; then down again to the old ship *Jhelum* (1855) for another; and then to Government Jetty for a third, sitting on an upturned ammunition box.

In this place the South wind, straight up from the Antarctic, is bitterly cold, but I was pleased to find that my preparations are (so far) equal to it and my fishing mittens allow me to use my hands for 10 minutes or so at a time. I've not yet had recourse to long pants, and my

Stage II Guernsey plus cardigan, but that may come. Everybody is in strictly functional clothing – very sensible too, though there are not many residents to be seen – mostly it's troops, in combat jackets, well-armed against the climate.

John Smith is seemingly the uncrowned king of marine antiquarians here, where there is the finest store of unexplored 19th century material still in existence. The best example, *Great Britain*, they have lost to Bristol! He thinks he is able to produce a mooring plan in which he noted down all the ships anchored in Port Stanley and Port William at the end of the campaign. Inter alia he produced a Bill of Sale and Registration Certificate for the 70ft schooner yacht *Pandora* built at Lymington in 185? given to him by Charles Nicholson (Campers). One of the later owners was a Naval Lieutenant who lived at Bartley Lodge in the New Forest which we once knew so well.

8/10/82

A wet morning, cold, but flying *is* taking place, and I'm sitting in a half-built Army-occupied house on the side of the harbour, one room of which is being used by the Army Air Corps as a sort of helicopter-passenger waiting-room, having been picked up from my digs by Nigel Maddox. My chopper is running half-hour late, so I can write up my account. The low hillside is a churned-up mass of debris over which you walk with the aid of duckboards; though I believe it was a building-site before war took over, so it was a mess to start with.

Rather late (1015 instead of 0900) an Army Air Corps Gazelle flitted down out of a rainstorm. In minutes I was aboard and away – no nonsense of helmets, etc just plug in headphones and away. Down to the harbour to look at P & O's subject, 5 minutes hover; *thump* down to refuel (3 mins) rotors still turning, then away along the coast to Fitzroy, 20 mins.

Another quick hover (in the wrong place as it turned out) and down to Fitzroy Settlement where 137 (Java) Battery RA under Major Tulloch are stationed in a variety of sheep-shearing buildings, ie shearers' bunkhouse – officer's and sergeants' mess, where I'm writing this at present. I made three exploring/painting drawing expeditions; the first on arrival, guided by Lt Steve Whitaker, RA who galloped me off a mile or so to see the Welsh Guards Memorial (loss of *Sir Galahad*), but I'd left my painting gear behind, not expecting this. After a good lunch (pretty hairy restaurant – a huge cavernous, draughty, sheep-shearing shed!) it snowed hard, but I had to return. This time it was a great success. The snow made a picture that wasn't there the am, even though I got rather damp. Later the snow cleared to show a marvellous scene of snow-covered distant mountains, running away to the east, with clouds throwing the light first here and then there.

9/10/82

At 0615 snow covers everything but only 2–3 ins. In a book on Falkland Birds I find dolphin gulls, a vulture, plover, an ashy-headed goose, all of which I've seen;

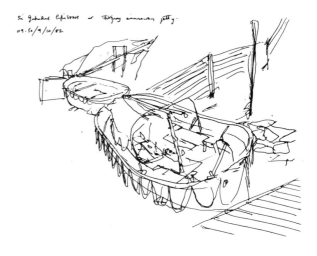

also kelp gulls, chiloe-widgeon and Falkland Thrush, which I've seen this morning.

David Maitland Mckgill Crichton, Captain 1st Queen's Own Highlanders met me at Goose Green, after I'd whisked away from Fitzroy by a helicopter (Scout this time) across East Falklands through snow squalls with sheep scattering beneath us as we went. It's now 2330 and I'm tucked up comfortably in my sleeping bag, my rucksack for a pillow, in a room totally empty except for the bedstead and mattress. After arrival he kindly drove me out to study the scene of the attack by 2 Para, and to their Memorial on the way back, close by the gorse line. The day continued squally, and the mountains looked fine as they came and went beneath the snow showers. In the evening I worked up some sketches and after supper the group of Highlanders were joined by a 'kelper', ex-British Antarctic Survey – an interesting, picturesque personality.

10/10/82

Awake 0630, beautiful morning. Wind W light. Walked over to the *Vicar of Bray*, perhaps the oldest complete Falkland wreck, now part of Goose Green pier. The way led along the shore past the sheep-dog kennels – *uproar*. They spend their lives mostly shut up, so a passer-by is a big moment.

On the other side of the inlet is an iron barque, *Garland*, derelict, but outwardly in good shape, apparently used by SAS as a spotting post during the recent war. The enemy never realised the fact, though I should think life aboard was tough for the SAS inmates though better than on a bare mountain.

Major Colin Gilmour and Captain Hugh McNair were my first contacts on arrival at Fox Bay East aboard HMS *Glasgow*'s Lynx, which had collected me from Goose Green. The latter met me, and the former toured me round the Argentinian defences of Fox Bay minefields at the usual smart military pace, which means nothing to them, but leaves me gasping and purple-faced. We did about three miles up to the perimeter, across and back again.

On return I was taken to Richard and Grizelda Cockwell's house – a very civilised, comfortable place,

like a big farmhouse. He is Manager of 15,000 acres in West Falkland, which is up for sale, so he is planning to go into local wool-yarn production. He is the son of an RE Colonel, and clearly a robust presence for any Argentinian to try to push about. He and his wife were most generous hosts and in the evening we stayed up late and talked a lot. He also took me out early on.

11/10/82

To see a penguin colony, before I was whisked off in *Glasgow*'s chopper to San Carlos Settlement to meet Lieutenant Nick Birch of 58 (Eyre's) Battery RA (His CO, Major Shahinian, was away).

Staff Sergeant Ferguson marched me off to visit a nearby Rapier Unit before lunch. I gave them the usual explanation of what I was up to, and at 3 pm I was due to 'yomp' up a neighbouring peak to visit another site while the weather is fine. I hope it stays that way, as the view from the top must be breath-taking. Those views I saw when in flight this morning were very fine indeed, coming along Falkland Sound – 'majestic, grand and aweful'. Meanwhile I have made a little sketch of what I saw this morning at Bombardier Day's Rapier Site. I've got to treat these things like watercolour vignettes, leaving lots of white for them to 'breathe'. It seems to suit this Falkland light.

pm   Nick Birch and I set off about 1500. (I'd done a little oil sketch by then of this morning's Rapier site). I borrowed a belt-pack to carry my small sketch-book as hefting my portfolio up 1500 feet or so only to find it too breezy to use the big pad, seemed a nonsense. We dressed carefully for the job as the weather can turn very awkward, and he was very considerate in his pacing. It took about 50 minutes of steady uphill work, mostly on tussocky grass and low heather, also a small, dark, fern, all of these clinging closely to the ground. The last part was very steep, until we reached the saddle, and traversed a few hundred yards to '23 Bravo' where Bombardier Spong's team had their Rapier site. Draughty as that mountain crest was, it enjoyed superb views in every direction, with distant snow showers blowing through from the south-west.

I drew; and the team busied themselves in

D. & E. Guns   137 Battery R.A.   The Sick mountains in the background

completing a handsome, galvanised-iron villa devised and erected by the Gurkha Engineers. Very snug it was, too, and its owners left me in no doubt that they enjoyed their independence as well as the view. Nobody to bother them, plenty of food, and an interesting task camouflaging and perfecting their eyrie among the granite and lime stone slabs.

About 1715 Birch and I set off for home, and supper. (A very good one it was too). Afterwards I walked out a mile or so to see the *Bahia Buen Suceso*, the Argentinian Naval Transport strafed by the Harriers in Fox Bay East, and now anchored here, deserted and no use to anyone. She is no beauty.

Back home at last light, somewhat puffed, but going well and no sore heels (so far).

23 Bravo six (Rapier) looking South East Gurkha Engineers build permanent Revetments for Rapier Crew.

12/10/82

Slept well, and stowed away a massive breakfast. Overcast morning, and even though the Falkland weather is so changeable, I'm glad I got round the area yesterday, especially the helo-trip in bright sun. This morning it would have been far less interesting.

These big bunk-houses at each settlement which accommodate the sheep-shearers are a blessing for the troops as the climate is not good for tents. At this time of year they are all empty. Not exactly three-star but effective enough. The Kelpers remind me of New Forest Commoners. Tough, adventurous, independent; tied by and to their grazing economy. Totally indifferent to the rest of the world and so-called progress. Their life-style is very easily supported because it's so very simple. All they eat is mutton, and excellent it is. The sheep-dogs eat mutton. Even the hens eat mutton. (When steam-engines were wanted out here in the War, their fire-boxes were adapted to

run on mutton, in the shape of sheep's hooves!). I don't know if they are happy, but I suspect they are (or were). If you like being left alone in plenty of space, every Falklander out in the island countryside (called 'camp') is a millionaire of freedom.

For the future, the Services are obviously here for a long while. Accommodation is being built at each of the Settlements for 2–300 men of the garrison force.

Clearly the place must change under this impact, which will alter the pattern of whatever social life there was. It can't have been exactly vivid. The Farm Manager here, I believe, visits Stanley once a year, only when he has to on business. It means a major expedition, and if I had the finest sea-trout fishing in the world and these surroundings for nothing on my doorstep, as he has, I daresay I would do the same.

During breakfast and afterwards, when I visited the Command Post (ie Ops Room in Naval terms) I found all hands coping with the consequence of a fire at '21

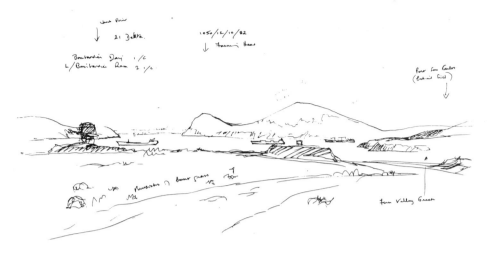

Charlie'. The new American cooker, installed by the Gurkha Engineers went on fire and burnt out the new hut. (Correction. The fire was *caused* by an Argentinian petrol heater which exploded, but it destroyed everthing *including* the American cooker, which would have created considerable worries had it been the cause). Nobody injured, fortunately, but, of course, this set the peat on the mountain top on fire, and without fire-brooms the crew could only stand and watch. One could see the smoke from down here at the Command Post, blowing away on the far side of the ridge. I proffered our New Forest design of Fire-Broom MK I as being a suitable supply item for all Rapier hill-top sites, at small cost to the Crown!

The weather, so dour this morning, with a strong w'ly wind, is tending to clear, but I've been lucky with it throughout, in my view, even (as at Fitzroy) when it snowed at the right minute. Also with my clothes and general preparations, which have all worked extremely well, much to my relief.

Up to 21 Delta site, to draw at leisure what I hurried through yesterday. Inspected the set-up, and got a lift back in the Postman's Land Rover. Then drew a pencil portrait of Corporal Dodds at work, he (i) having fed me well, and (ii) urged me to do it. He's a small, lively man and a first-class cook who keeps everyone happy. His cooking range is a monster, designed to burn peat, and this it does very well, but it creates a vast amount of ash. Unless this is cleared from the flues frequently you can't get the oven to heat properly; but when clean it's an absolute furnace.

The peat used for fuel is sometimes cut nowadays by a type of specialised bulldozer-cum-dicing machine. You just climb on, drive to a nearby hill-top or wherever, dig what you want, fork-lift it into a trailer and come bucketing back home, down a one-in-four

hillside. The longer you keep it, the better fuel it becomes. Six years and it's about right! (Usually it's burned in about one or two). The wind, which is such a local feature, dries it very quickly. At every Settlement there is an open-sided 'shed'. *Penelope* (the 50ft island ferry-boat at Goose Green, with pens for sheep on her deck) had half a sheep hung up in her starboard rigging. Apparently the birds (vultures, etc) can't settle on it, so it sits there quite happily until wanted. Only in summer, sometimes, the flies prove a bother. (Windmills ought to work well here, but I've seen none).

Down this pm to *Bahia Buen Suceso*. Borrowed binoculars (vg indeed) which allowed me to draw her satisfactorily from a mile away in the shelter of a shed. It's blowing a gale, bitterly cold, so this was a real saving in energy and calories, as well as time. The wind out here blows tirelessly, but near the Farm Manager's house he (or his predecessors, more likely) have piled peat-banks to give a shelter-belt for gorse and some hardy coniferous trees to grow, where I found a family of sheep enjoying the lee.

Staff Sergeant Ferguson has just looked in to tell me I'm to be on parade for the chopper at 0930 tomorrow morning.

Everyone, throughout, has been ceaselessly kind and considerate bar only, perhaps, in their use of high-speed over the ground; but that is second nature to them, and so it should be. It's 1745 and I've tidied up my pictures, etc. The wind is roaring in the dusk outside my window, and, snow has blotted out the landscape. What *luck* I've had to see *so* much, *so* easily, compared with how things might have been. I was bothered, too, in case I found life out here with the Army in these harsh conditions too tough (in fact it's been no difficulty at all) but if one disregards the inevitably rough side of it (and it really is inevitable, for they are all on active service at full Alert all the time) the morale is high, the atmosphere thoroughly cheerful, and the hardship due more to the climate and extempore living conditions than anything else. No wonder the heather clings to the ground, and is burnt black by the salt wind, ditto the little fern-like plant, which never dares to raise it's fronds.

I believe I have seen about half the Falkland birds, but without the book I can't be sure. It makes me feel like Darwin himself. He was here only about 150 years ago, and now I've seen both Darwin and Fitzroy, which bear their names. How amazed they'd have been at all these events!

13/10/82

0630   called by Corporal Dodds with a cup of tea. A lovely morning, wind light, and sky crystal clear. After the usual massive breakfast I packed myself for travel. (Helicopters are often late, for many good reasons; but sometimes they're early, and can't be kept waiting!). The Command Post had a quiet night after yesterday and last night's activities. Vehicles, mostly Land Rovers, are continually getting bogged in around the place. Last night there were two such, quite late in the evening.

I did a quick drawing of the Command Post in action, as this completes the picture of Rapier activity, and covers the job done by my immediate hosts, here at HQ.

I shall be really sorry to leave. My time has been so short, but this has made me work to the limit, physically as well as at my job.

At 0905 (not 0930) the Wessex arrived, and I was ready for it, chatting to the Gurkha Engineer Sergeant on the airfield about his building programme. Quiet, with an immobile face that suddenly flashes into a brilliant smile.

Whoosh, off again, up to Port San Carlos air-strip, site of the first Harrier landing, then on – right across the island, passing close to Teal Inlet and latterly along the path of the 3 Brigade's advance to Stanley. All the famous peaks in sight, Kent, Two Sisters, Tumbledown, etc – amazing, absolutely.

Down below the land sweeps away for miles; slow curves of camel-coloured grass, peaty ponds, and the occasional sign of man, such as a fence or a shepherd's hut. These huts are about 12ft by 8ft, like a little Noah's

0758/13/10/82   Command Post 58 Eyres Battery. San Carlos Settlement.

Ark, built of galvanised sheet, with a chimney, the whole of which sits on a big sledge and gets towed out 10–15 miles or more across country, there to sit, miles from anywhere (until it is wanted somewhere else).

The sledge is an Island invention, strongly-built of timber on two longitudinal, steel-shod runners, with a towing bracket in front. This creates a platform on which anything (peat, stores, maiden-aunts or whatever) can be loaded, and towed by the big 'Island tractors' up or down the steep slopes, or across country.

Only a Kelper can do this effectively, and even he gets bogged down. The big difference is that he can tell from the feel of his progress, and the look of the ground what tactics to use, and which way to go. The very few tracks are easily made impassable at bottle-necks if too many vehicles make use of them, as the fragile surface of the peat, once cut, is quickly churned to mincemeat, and there's nothing but a soggy mass for the wheels to grip on. This type of driving skill is like that developed by driving on sand in the Western Desert in WW II.

Back at Stanley, met by Nigel Maddox, and found David Young BBC at John Smith's. Walked out to draw in the afternoon, and when I returned I found Norman Grummet, provider of 'instant houses' (50 of them) here on a visit on inspection, also Stewart Campbell, War Graves Commission, who'd arrived at John Smith's the day I left. (In fact he took over my bed here rather as I took over Cranley Onslow's at Fox Bay East). We talked late about the Islands, war, etc.

14/10/82

0645 Turn out, hard w'ly wind and rain. Walked up to the Secretariat to make my number with Captain Dobson Royal Navy, SNO Falklands and General Thorne GOC, both extremely nice and interested in what I had to show; ditto John Chandler and his colleague at Government House, where I went later to 'sign the book'. Unfortunately, the Governor (now Sir Rex Hunt) was away till afternoon.

At 1100 I met David Young at the British Forces Broadcasting studio, which he's been repairing and refitting. A colleague interviewed me for 15 minutes on my visit and work, to be edited down to about five minutes for transmission here, and on other Forces networks elsewhere in the world.

Back to lunch, and to pack for 1430 collection, until phoned to delay until 2030; so afterwards I studied John Smith's splendid library of Falklands books, to try to fill out the bones of my slender knowledge.

At 2030 I was collected by Nigel Maddox and driven to the airport (I'm to phone his wife on my return) and then stood for two hours among 50 or so others on the way home. A comfortless but, to me, very interesting wait, to see all three Services and ranks intermingled. How easily they do it. When the moment came, we boarded the Hercules in time-coloured style, jammed like sardines, but willing and good-natured ones. Three medical cases on stretchers, plus RAF medical staff. Urrrrr, Urrrrr, and off we go into the night, 'undo seat

NO SMOKING

1615/15/10/82

belts' and (where I'm sitting amidships) 'off sweaters' too. It's boiling hot beneath the heating ducts. 4–5 hours of restless discomfort before I scramble out over the dozing corpses, and make myself some coffee. Dawn is just breaking; we are four miles up over a vast, empty South Atlantic strewn with random cloud below us. (Funny to think in the mid-1850's the sea below us was as full of shipping as the Channel is today).

I stand, or sit on a box, or peer out of a porthole for the next 3½ hours; then breakfast (Pack – A type = tinned potato salad, plus beef loaf, etc.) then, realising I'm unlikely ever to do this again, out sketch-book – two line drawings of hangar and cockpit, which takes the time up to near Ascension. As I scramble back to my seat from visiting the flight deck, my neighbour is interested; happily so, as it turns out later on.

Thump down on Ascension's runway, and a blast of heat as the doors are opened. Over to the passenger hangar, fill in next-of-kin form and (Oh, blessings!) the VC 10 has been held up for us. We can fly directly to Brize Norton – not even Dakar for fuel.

It's a warmish wait, but during it I meet some Naval staff from *Illustrious*, Lt-Commanders Cullen and Billson (who remembered me aboard *Bristol* with David Brown).

All aboard for BN, off across the blazing tarmac, ¼ mile, me loaded like a camel as (unlike the others) I dare not lose sight of my stuff. (They put theirs on a baggage tray, with wheels).

I got a window seat, like last time, and it's 'fasten seat-belts' and away. I think everyone slept a little, after 12 hours of Hercules. Food came, and went. Plenty of it, but insubstantial stuff somehow. It was a comatose, dull trip, much of it in the dark, and latterly

my right foot became very swollen and painful – can't blame it – it's been stood on, or overheated, or both, since 2130 last night, 24 hours.

Nothing in sight, except a few stars, until shortly before landing at Brize Norton when one could being to see golden, misty shapes below, like scattered galaxies, focused on town and city centres; all lit, I suppose, for Friday night in a civilised world; so remote from those Islands I've just left, which are still barely 'settled' in the 19th century, and are so hard for the 20th to understand.

On landing it turns out that my neighbour in the Hercules was Brian Smith; scientist, from REME at Christchurch, it transpired. Would I like a lift home? His driver is waiting for him. Would I? You bet I would!

After a long Custom/baggage delay (amazing, 600 miles in one hour, 60 yards in the next one) and I find myself about midnight en route for home, doggie and my Jean, who came up on the phone the moment I called, bless her. She was all set to drive up right away to fetch me, but this lift home is far better.

All around me had been relatives and families, patiently awaiting fellow passengers, some absent since mid-summer, some, I feel sure, seeing their new-born children for the first time. That must be quite a moment. I've just seen one father (a Naval Petty Officer) peer in delighted wonderment at his wife's present to him, all wrapped up in woolly clothes – her first I suspect, by the way he looked at them both.

So there it is. Thrilled to go. Thrilled to get back. If life holds more, it can't be for me – (or, perhaps, for him?).

Postscript

In May 1985 I returned once more via RAF to the Falklands to continue painting for the Armed Forces but also to study and record for our industrial contractors the opening of the new Mount Pleasant Airport. Flying out by Hercules from Ascension, this time I joined RFA *Diligence* at Stanley, and on a lowering day of strong wind we sailed round into Falkland Sound from the North, to enter San Carlos Water and moor close to Ajax Bay and the two buoys which mark the last resting place of HMS *Antelope*. At dusk that evening I stood on the wing of the bridge while the light faded from the sky, testing in my mind's eye the accuracy of my earlier recollections in paint of my visit in 1982. As may be imagined I had other thoughts, too, at seeing again this scene of such remarkable endeavour and extraordinary success.

This time the widespread debris of war had largely disappeared, but though the slit-trenches had been filled in, life still had to be lived against a military background. All travellers arriving continue to be warned against the dangers of uncleared mines and booby-traps. Even so, the large proportion of the islands remains unaltered by the Argentinian invasion.

The following dawn was one of great splendour, calm and lovely. This allowed me to get ashore easily to land at the Ajax Bay jetty to sketch the site of the Field Hospital set up by the Royal Army Medical Corps in the abandoned buildings close by. Later that day I flew South and East over Darwin and Goose Green to land at the newly-constructed Airport at Mount Pleasant.

This civil engineering feat set up several unlikely records. In distance from supply sources, absence of facilities, harshness of climate and remoteness from civilisation, the site of Mount Pleasant must challenge most comers.

The ability to handle wide-bodied civil aircraft in the Falklands had long been seen as desirable by all who knew the place, in particular by Lord Shackleton's 1976 and 1982 Reports; but the will and means was lacking until the Argentinian invasion. This made clear, also the essential need for a strategic airfield able to operate fixed-wing fighter aircraft to defend the islands against such attacks.

The joint consequence of these two demands was this new Airport. It was operating in record time, a mere 18 months from the start. To do this the civilian work-force faced and overcame handicaps and complications very similar (bar being shot at) to those of the soldiers, sailors and airmen who had fought and won the 1982 campaign.

The basic survey of the Airport site was originally the work of the Royal Engineers, carried out at the end of the campaign when the urgent need for it was clear beyond doubt; and to arrange it would at one time have been within their competence. But today the scale of the enterprise was too large, consequently the surveys requirements were put out to civil engineering tender. The construction was tendered for successfully by Joint Venture of Laing, Mowlem and Amey Roadstone (LMA).

The small nucleus of this now-vast enterprise arrived at the barren East Cove, seven miles away, aboard the specially adapted 13,000-ton merchant ship *Merchant Providence*; and from there the bulldozers first pushed a road inland seven miles to the Airport site, then a further four miles up to the quartzite quarries; while another branch swung away eastwards across bog and moor and mountain for thirty miles to Stanley. Meanwhile the *Merchant Providence* became the Island's first permanent, *deep*-water, moored pontoon/wharf, and thus the bridge across which passed every single piece of equipment and machinery to reach its task ashore. It was the classic Falkland Harbour solution – 1983 version.

At the time I was there I found the Mount Pleasant Airport village of some 2000 men and 300 women all working like beavers; the one thought uppermost in their minds was the timely completion of their task. Nobody pretended it was much fun sloshing around in pelting rain in an ocean of ubiquitous pallid mud. (Nor, I surmise, in its summer counterpart, the cloud of dust which, until the roads are tarmac, pursues every moving lorry and truck).

Apart from the welfare provisions, canteens, etc. on site, there was nowhere outside the construction camps to go to relax socially. Stanley, 30 miles away over the newly-constructed and still unfinished road, was out of bounds. Mount Pleasant was a place to work, and mighty little else; but that suited them. It was what they had signed on for. Coming as I did straight from our tetchy, querulous 1985 Britain, I found the unifying atmosphere just as I had in 1982, as invigorating as champagne.

To many there, I was just a strange creature, an artist, asking silly questions, but no matter what my problem, everyone seemed to rejoice in their ability to cope with it. As a result, and despite some crippling weather which relented with unbelievable luck for only just a vital hour or so in the course of several days, I was able to see and draw everything I wanted to.

Especially helpful was James Hamilton, ('Hammy' to his friends) a hefty Scottish foreman-transport-driver. In the enormous cab of his truck we scaled the heights of Mount Pleasant to reach the Amey Roadstone quartzite quarry on its crest. The ponderous 10-geared machine swayed like a ship at sea as we wound our way up the glistening slippery mountain-side track. If we lose traction and stop, it means a slide backwards to the foot of the slope . . . but Hammy was a musician. Every time his truck began an elephantine waltz of its own his feet and hands, moving deftly like those of a cathedral organist, re-exerted their control.

Once on the mountain-top the driver's cab, high above the ground, made a wonderful artist's studio. Warm and dry behind the huge, panorama windscreen we were sheltered from the brisk mountain-top winds. Beneath us we could see for miles to where the distant Airport buildings squatted squarely around the ribbon of the airstrip. When I scrambled out to scale the nearby granite peak, considerate Hammy came too, to make certain his queer ward came to no harm.

The next day he kindly arranged for one of his colleagues, Alistair Maclean, to drive me along the new Stanley road the 15 miles out to Bluff Cove aboard a daily 4500 gallon water-tanker, first cousin to his own truck. This allowed me for the first time to see at ground level (instead of from the air) the terrain which in 1982 the infantry of 5 Brigade had had to cross towards Stanley, and, in particular, the route followed by the 1st Battalion Welsh Guards who had bivouacked near Bluff Cove on 10 June before continuing their advance. Below and alongside us as we drove from time to time ran fast-flowing streams and rivers, swirling seawards through the brown, rolling landscape. Far to the south a luminous sea-horizon was broken by distant rain-squalls drifting across from the direction of Cape Horn; to the north loomed the craggy outlines of the Wickham Heights lightly dusted with snow. And all the time the four winds blew, and blew, and blew. . .

That evening, as we returned to the throbbing scene of activity at Mount Pleasant Airport, I ruminated on the early pioneer days of the 1850 Gold Rush whose ships had fought their way westwards passed the Falklands out to California and gone eastwards to Australia. This was a new reminder of the vitality of the British in exporting its most vigorous and enterprising growth of citizens to explore and develop so much of the world before returning it, and their administration, to the original inhabitants. Whatever the failures of Empire, in time the long view of history would surely come to judge it as a story of creative success.

In the last 150 years the life of the Falkland Islanders has come into prominence only three times, when war has broken briefly and dramatically into their picturesque tranquility. The sole reason has been their Island's geographical significance, like a British sentry-box placed at Cape Horn.

That happy isolation is now at an end; active measures foreseen by the Shackleton Reports must now follow to support and stabilise the islands and to realise their potentialities, for possession of the Falklands is central to all British influence and aspiration in the area.

The opening of this southernmost Airport in the world could well lead to trans-Antarctic air travel by wide-bodied jets, able to reach New Zealand and Australia, some 5–6,000 miles away, on a Great Circle course.

The waters of the great southern seas are prolific fishing grounds; to control them by licence from the Falklands would be highly profitable. Such considerations have long been pondered, and now there are many new ones: but whatever the future may hold, one thing can be predicted with absolute certainty: Over the Falklands the winds will still blow, and blow, and blow . . .

Appendix

The outcome was a success for the LMA partnership. Meanwhile the creation of a permanent harbour wharf at Mare Harbour in East Cove, sited just astern of the 'Merchant Providence', was entrusted to the partnership of Wimpey/Taylor Woodrow/Sir Alex Gibb and Partners. The supporting firms included the best that the country could provide, names known the world over. They include the following:

NOMINATED SUBCONTRACTORS:

Balfour Kilpatrick Limited	Mechanical and Electrical Supply and Installation
GEC/Ruston Diesels Limited	Main Power Generation Supply and Installation
McTay Limited	Fuel Tankage Supply System and Installation

MAJOR SUBCONTRACTORS & SUPPLIERS:

Cenargo Limited	Cargo Shipping
Cunard Shipping Services Limited	Passenger Shipping
Cunard Crusader World Travel Limited	Passenger Air Travel
General Navigation and Commerce Company Limited	Packing and Freight Forwarders
Hallam Group of Nottingham PLC	Building Supply and Erection
Kelvin Catering (Camps) Limited	Camp Catering and Administration
Ward Brothers (Sherburn) Limited	Steelframe Design and Construct
Wyesplan Limited	Building Supply and Erection
Armco Limited	Culverts
Aveling-Barford Limited	Construction Plant
Beechdale Engineering Limited	Roadforms and Cover Frames

Beeswift Limited	Protective Clothing
Berkeley JCB Limited	Construction Plant
Blaw Knox Construction Equipment Company	Construction Plant
Blue Circle Industries PLC	Cement
Bowmaker (Plant) Ltd now Finning Limited	Construction Plant
BP Aquaseal Limited	Construction Plant
Cable and Wireless PLC	Communication Equipment
Compactors Engineers Limited	Construction Plant
Compair Holman Limited	Construction Plant
Degremont Laing Limited	Water and Sewage Treatment
Dynapac (UK) Limited	Construction Plant
Empire Furnishing Company	Furniture, Camp Accommodation
Esso Petroleum Company Limited	Fuel and Lubricants
Frederick Parker plc	Construction Plant
George Cohen Machinery Limited	Workshop Buildings
Goodwin Barsby	Construction Plant
Grove Cranes	Construction Plant
Johnston Pipes Limited	GRP and Concrete Pipes
Lancer Boss Limited	Forklift Trucks
Leigh Land Reclamation Limited	Asphalt Sand
Lenantons Limited	Timber
Leyland Vehicles Exports Limited	Construction Plant
Mining Machinery Developments Limited	Construction Plant
OTR Tyres Ltd	Tyres
W H Perry Limited	Construction Plant
Petbow Limited	Construction Plant
Tripower Limited	Temporary Electrics
Yorkshire Plastics International	UPVC Pipes and Fittings

HANDOVER IN SAN CARLOS WATER 11/6/85   'AVENGER', 'DILIGENCE' AND 'BRAZEN'   DAVID COBB.

H.M.S. Coventry
20, 21.

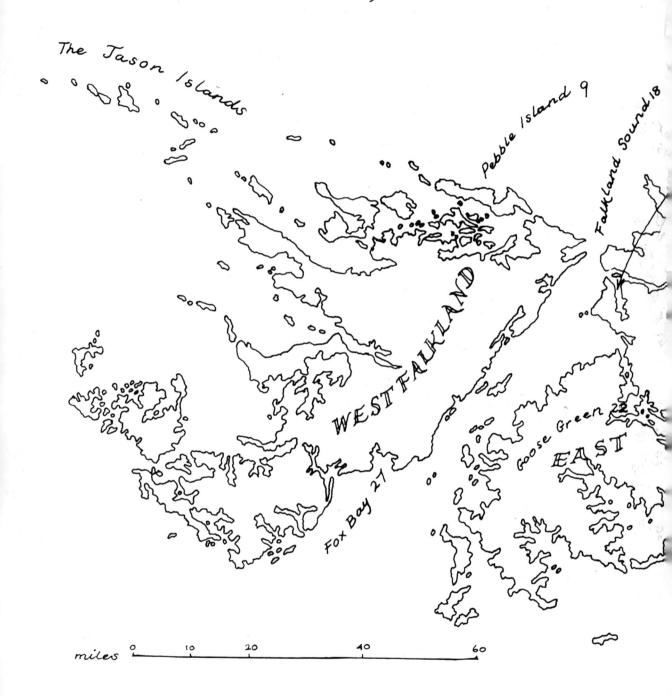

The Jason Islands

Pebble Island 9

Falkland Sound 18

WEST FALKLAND

Goose Green 22

EAST

Fox Bay 21

miles   0   10   20   40   60

Numerals denote numbered illustrations.

-- jean main cobb ..